THE FINAL EXAM
PREPARING FOR THE JUDGMENT

Published in 2023 by Connor Court Publishing Pty Ltd

Copyright © John Flader 2023

All rights reserved. No part of this book may be reproduced or transmitted in any form or by any means, electronic or mechanical, including photo copying, recording or by any information storage and retrieval system, without prior permission in writing from the publisher.

Connor Court Publishing Pty Ltd
PO Box 7257
Redland Bay QLD 4165
sales@connorcourt.com
www.connorcourt.com

Printed in Australia

ISBN: 9781922815330

Front cover designed by Mathew De Sousa

Photo credit: Dennis Jarvis/Wikimedia Commons, CC BY-SA 2.0

Scripture citations are from the Revised Standard Version, Second Catholic Edition, Ignatius Edition, of the Bible, copyrighted 2006, by the Division of Christian Education of the National Council of Churches in the United States of America, and are used by permission. All rights reserved.

We've all taken tests before, whether we were ready or not. Nobody who reads this book will be unprepared for the one test that matters most, the ultimate final exam that will determine how we spend eternity. We will all be judged. In *The Final Exam* Dr Flader explains not only why that judgment is fitting and necessary, but also why it's good. The perfect sequel to *Dying to Live* — highly recommended.

Scott Hahn PhD, Founder and President, St Paul Center, Scanlan Professor of Theology, Franciscan University of Steubenville.

The Hebrew midwives refuse to obey the king's order to kill any male child they deliver. Mother Teresa instructs a Muslim gentleman to 'kindly build a mosque' for lepers in Yemen who need somewhere to pray. The young priest left a quadriplegic after a car accident says, "I feel like a millionaire who has lost a thousand dollars!". You do not need to be a Catholic or even a Christian to find *The Final Exam* instructive. It's an account of the judgment at the end of life which has something in it for both believers and unbelievers. For the idea of preparing for the judgment is not only a matter of living so as to please God – it is also the idea of living life to the full! I recommend this short account of the way that Christian teachings complement the best of secular convictions.

Dr Bernadette Tobin AO, GCSG, Director, Plunkett Centre for Ethics, Australian Catholic University, St Vincent's Health Network & Calvary Healthcare.

At a time when the world desperately needs clarity on natural law and ethics, Dr John Flader has offered – with courage, grace and humility – the very insights needed. This book saves the reader decades of heavy reading and research. Dr Flader, intelligently and engagingly, pulls together vital threads of philosophy, theology and common sense, generously giving us a comprehensive, yet readily understandable, useful book that one can dip into, again and again. Anyone looking for answers to the deeper questions in life, will find that this book has something to offer each and every one of us.

Sophie York, BA, LLB, Dip Leg Prac., Lecturer in Law, Sydney University, Adjunct Lecturer in Law, University of Notre Dame Australia.

Modern life is busy, fragmented, full of distractions and contradictory voices. A growing number of people lack opportunities to think deeply about the moral life, with many never having Christian moral teaching properly explained and proposed to them. Others might have heard it all before but find themselves questioning or complacent about the meaning and value of individual choices and actions.

In *The Final Exam,* Dr Flader presents a practical and positive guide to living our "best life" now and for eternity. He emphasises that the moral life needs more than our passing attention. Instead, it needs to be studied, reflected upon, and ultimately lived with freedom and love.

The *Final Exam* explores foundational concepts such as the objective nature of morality, freedom and conscience, virtues and vices, sin and repentance, justice and mercy. It also explains *why* and *how* following the precepts of the Ten Commandments is a reasonable and fulfilling way of living and acting, for people of all faiths and of none.

Just as God's promise of eternal life is for everyone, this book is written in a way that is accessible and inviting to everyone. Dr Flader explains the harmony between the universal natural moral law and Christian moral teaching, encouraging every person to embrace a grace-led life in accordance with these teachings. Not everyone will agree with everything in this book; but its content is proposed with sensitivity, respect and charity.

Whether you are curious, conflicted, in need of personal encouragement, or just hoping to learn more, this is recommended reading for your "final exam", and certainly not something to risk leaving until the week before the exam!

Dr Brigid McKenna MBBS, MBioeth, GradCert ULT, FHEA
Coordinator Clinical Practice and Medical Ethics, Tasmanian School of Medicine.

A sequel to *Dying to Live – Reflections on Life After Death,* Dr Flader's new book is an accessible and crisp reflection on human morality and "the good life" from within the Christian tradition. How well have I lived? Who do I want to be in the end? In *The Final Exam,* the author invites the reader to delve into these questions with his down-to-earth explanation of core Christian teachings, and their links with ideas from antiquity. He has done a masterful job of showing how the Ten Commandments are not just part of the Judaeo-Christian tradition, but are rather based on the natural law and hence valid for all. The book's logical structure and conversational style reflect the author's many decades of work with students of all ages, as well as his training in Canon Law.

Jeremy Prichard BA (Hons.), BA, LLB, PhD, Professor of Criminal Law, University of Tasmania

True happiness comes predominantly not from self-gratification, but from fidelity to a worthy purpose. In both *Dying to Live* and *The Final Exam* Dr Flader gently invites you to recommit to this spirit and principle, in both your life and your work. Here he writes again with the same lucidity and simplicity, that are so powerful that even a child could read it and an adult be transformed by it. His "fatherly" advice will help prepare you for a *summa cum laude* outcome in the "Final Exam", which will surely encourage you to *Carpe Deum*! and not just *Diem*!, and to live every day of your life in homage to God, rather than as a hostage to your own ego.

Sergio Maresca, Mentor, Life Coach, Speaker, Author

As a university lecturer, I give my students all the information and resources they need to excel. After that, it is up to the students themselves to do the work. Sadly, I have often seen students who did not work hard come to the exam with anxiety and regret at the time wasted, thinking of the loss of what might have been. If this is the case for a university exam, where failure may not be the end, how much more important it is for everyone to make use of the resources God has given them to live a good life and so be well prepared for life's final exam, where failure is truly the end. *The Final Exam* beautifully and coherently presents a summary of the most important teachings of God on the good life, preparing the reader to face God in the judgment. The book is practical and easy to read, and it incorporates the how to live as well as the why. This exceptional book is inspirational and motivational, and I highly recommend it to everyone who wants to "get it right" and pass the most important exam of all.

Louise McDonald, RN, Grad Cert (Chronic Health Conditions), Certified Lifestyle Coach, Lecturer in Bioscience, QUT.

In memory of my parents, who brought me up to believe in God and in life after death, and set me firmly on the way to heaven, where I hope to meet them one day.

Contents

Foreword	13
Introduction	15
1 Preparing for the Final Exam	17
2 Objective morality	23
Human rights	24
Natural justice	25
Crimes against humanity	26
The natural law	26
Characteristics of the natural law	28
The natural law in the ancient world	31
Sophocles	31
Aristotle	32
Cicero	33
Human laws and the natural law	35
Moral absolutes	36
3 Foundations of moral life	41
Human freedom	41
Conscience	44
Virtues and vices	46
Emotions	50
Sin	51
Temptations	53
4 The value of suffering	57
The suffering of Jesus Christ	59
1. Suffering strengthens character	61
2. Suffering helps one to be more sympathetic towards others who are suffering	63
3. Suffering brings people closer to God	64
4. Suffering is a manifestation of God's love	66
5. Suffering can help to make up for our sins	67
6. Suffering can be offered up for others	68
7. Suffering benefits the carers	69

5 The worship of God — 73
- The Ten Commandments — 73
- The first commandment — 74
- The second commandment — 79
- The third commandment — 81

6 Love for our neighbour — 85
- Love for strangers and "enemies" — 86
- Forgiving others — 89
- Avoiding prejudices — 91
- Putting ourselves out for others — 92

7 Honour your father and your mother — 97
- Duties of children towards their parents — 98
- Duties of parents towards their children — 100
- Rights and duties in civil society — 101

8 You shall not kill — 103
- Murder — 104
- Abortion — 105
- Euthanasia — 106
- Suicide — 107
- Exceptions to the wrongfulness of killing — 108
- Giving scandal — 109
- Neglecting health — 110

9 You shall not commit adultery — 111
- Sexuality and marriage — 111
- The virtue of chastity — 112
- Offences against chastity — 114
- Openness to life and contraception — 117
- Offences against the dignity of marriage — 122

10 You shall not steal — 125
- Justice — 125
- Respect for the property of others — 126
- Restitution — 128

Care for the environment	129
11 You shall not bear false witness	**131**
Respect for the truth	131
Offences against the truth	133
Offences against the reputation of another	134
Rash judgment	134
Detraction	135
Slander	136
Revealing secrets	137
12 You shall not covet	**139**
You shall not covet your neighbour's wife	139
You shall not covet your neighbour's goods	141
13 The final exam	**145**
We must be sorry for our sins	145
We will be judged by how we have used the gifts God has given us	148
God knows us better than we know ourselves	150
God will take into account what we knew or did not know about his law	152
Getting closer to God	155

Foreword

Study is a virtue, whatever one thinks of exams. A student who has studied can answer questions with confidence; a student who has not does not know where to start.

The moral life is, of course, no mere academic exercise. But there is such a thing as moral truth, and there are clear moral principles by which we can assess the morality of human acts. In many ways the story of modernity is a story of a loss of confidence in the existence and intelligibility of objective morality.

Some believe that morality is reducible to one's personal reflection on the good life. This may go some way to explaining the value placed on first-person experience in contemporary public debate. This is, however, a perilous idea. The passions can go hopelessly astray if not guided by reason. Reason, for its part, can easily go astray if it is not anchored in a tradition. Indeed, there is no such thing as rational reflection in a vacuum – human reason always seeks support in tradition. Regrettably, for many today, that tradition is postmodern relativism. Alternatively, one might adopt an Enlightenment skepticism whereby the pursuit of wisdom is replaced with an inordinate desire for certitude.

The philosophers of Ancient Greece and Rome had a far greater appreciation of the meaning and value of wisdom. Practical wisdom or *phronesis* was a cornerstone of Aristotle's ethics, to provide one notable example. Indeed, for Aristotle, a life of virtue *just is* the good life. Some degree of wealth and social success will help you, but ultimately human beings flourish through rational activity in accord with virtue.

Yet even the great thinkers of antiquity were limited in their ability to grasp the full content of the moral life. It was only with the advent of Christianity in the West that we began to fully appreciate foundational civilisational values such as the dignity of the human person and the importance of care for society's most vulnerable members. One might also add Catholic teaching on human sexuality, given the role it plays in ensuring strong families and lasting marriage.

All of which is to say, one does well to seriously study the riches of Christian insight into the moral life. It is here that the following pages will be especially useful. To my mind, *The Final Exam* is an eminently clear articulation of Catholic teaching on the moral life. John Flader provides a concise, accessible and lucid account of Catholic teaching on the morality of actions, freedom, conscience, the emotions, and virtue, and also summarises the main moral teachings of Catholic Christianity arising from the decalogue.

One can almost hear the inimitable voice of the author echoing through these pages as he guides us through some of the most vexed questions of Christian morality and communicates to us the joy of Christian life and the ultimate lightness of the commandments, which are a blueprint for human flourishing rather than an unnatural constraint on our desires.

One of the greatest strengths of this book is its clarity. Despite the complex nature of some of its themes, the author manages to provide a clear picture of why the Church is committed to the moral positions that it holds, and why anyone sincerely open to the truth and common sense ought to see in Catholic moral theology a sound account of how we can most fully realise those capacities that make us human – in particular, reason and freedom.

At a time when it seems that many actors in the public square are intent on obscuring foundational truths about the human person, John Flader's *The Final Exam* is a very welcome contribution.

Dr Xavier Symons, PhD, Human Flourishing Program,
Institute for Quantitative Social Science, Harvard University

Introduction

My previous book *Dying to Live,* of which the present one is a sequel, was not my idea, as I explained in the introduction. The idea came from a friend, who suggested a book about life after death for people who didn't believe in it. The present one was not my idea either. At least as regards whether the book would be written at all. This time the idea came from a friend who really liked *Dying to Live* and who asked me to write another book in the same style. I thanked him for the invitation but didn't give it another thought. I had no intention of writing another book and, what is more, I don't have time to write books.

About a month later, I was thinking of his suggestion and it occurred to me that if there were a topic for which I had already written quite a bit, it might be worth considering. This thought soon led to the idea of writing a development of the final chapter of *Dying to Live,* "What must I do?" That chapter gives a few ideas on how to live in order to prepare for the judgment at the end of life. But a more thorough treatment of moral life would be highly advisable to prepare anyone to meet their Maker in the judgment. I had already written quite a bit on that topic in my book *Journey into Truth,* which came out in 2014. That book, with its accompanying set of DVDs, explains the Catholic faith for people who might consider entering the Church, or who are already in it and want to go deeper in their understanding. Part of that book is on moral life, on how to live in order to do what is right and avoid what is wrong. So I now had a topic and some material with which to start.

But how do you write a book when you don't have time? I guess the answer lies in the common experience we all have that you can always find time for something you really want to do. I wanted to write this book and so I took advantage of all the spare hours and minutes I could find. I gave myself six months to do it, and surprised myself by finishing it in four months.

The Final Exam is an extensive development of some of the ideas in the last chapter of *Dying to Live*. It proposes to help the reader come to know in greater detail how to live in order to please God and prepare for the judgment. And living well is important, not only to prepare for the next life, but to live this one to the full. After all, we will only find the happiness and well-being we seek when we live well. Most of us have a general idea of what is right and wrong, but this present book gives a much more detailed and comprehensive understanding of it.

It deals with questions like whether morality is objective or rather subjective, dependent on how each person sees it. Also, questions like the role of conscience, the influence of emotions on moral life, the role of virtues, the value of suffering, and so on.

Like *Dying to Live,* this book is addressed to people of all religious persuasions and of none. I draw on the Bible and on Christian ethics, particularly those of the Catholic Church, because, as I explained in that earlier book, that Church has two thousand years of existence, it was founded by Jesus Christ himself, and its teachings make sense. Not to mention the fact that the Catholic Church is the largest single religious denomination in the world, and more than half of all Christians are Catholics.

Naturally, you don't need to be Catholic or Christian in order to go to heaven. As I explained in *Dying to Live,* the Catholic Church teaches that anyone can go to heaven, as long as they strive to lead a good life and are sincerely sorry for their sins.

So, without further explanation, I invite you to sit back, relax, and enjoy reading at your leisure. I hope you find in this book some helpful guidelines to live your life to the full and be well prepared for the judgment, the final exam.

1

Preparing for the Final Exam

We have all taken lots of exams. We were introduced to them, perhaps with some degree of fear and trembling, in primary school, then came more in secondary school and possibly later in some form of tertiary education. Apart from these, there were exams to gain a driver's licence and who knows how many more.

In general, they were pretty important. At least we thought so at the time. And they were increasingly important as we advanced on our educational path. If we failed to pass, we could generally take the exam again until we finally passed. Or maybe it didn't make any difference and we could continue with our studies. In the worst case scenario, we could give up and pursue some other course of study. Many people have made multiple such changes in their life. When all is said and done, failing an exam is not the end of the world.

But there is one exam that is. It is the end of the world – for us, at least. That exam is, of course, the last exam we will ever take, the final exam. The one we take when we die and face God in the judgment. That one is the most important, because we can take it only once, and if we fail, we remain separated from God forever by our own free choice. We saw this in *Dying to Live*.

And don't get me wrong – that final exam, the judgment, is for real. For everyone, no matter whether they believe in it or not. The atheist, the agnostic, the believer in some religion or in none will all see their life played out before them in the moment they die. And they will see immediately whether they have passed, in which case they will be on their way to eternal life with God in heaven, or whether they have failed and are on their way to eternal separation from God and damnation.

Maybe you say you don't care what I write in this book about the judgment and life after death. You simply don't believe in it and you will take your chances. Okay, but that is a risk I personally would not be prepared to take. There is too much at stake. I invite you to apply the reasoning of Pascal's Wager, which we considered in the second chapter of *Dying to Live*, the chapter titled "Placing a bet". Either there is life after death or there isn't. The person who does not believe should ask himself or herself: Am I certain there is no life after death? Am I perhaps gambling that there isn't, with the risk of being wrong? If I am wrong, I stand to lose everything, everything, and for all eternity. Can I afford to take that risk? Would it not be better to assume that there, at least, might be life after death, and a judgment, and live my life accordingly?

What is more, Jesus Christ, the founder of the largest single religion on earth assured us there is life after death. He told Martha, a woman whose brother Lazarus had died four days before, "Your brother will rise again... I am the resurrection and the life; he who believes in me, though he die, yet shall he live, and whoever lives and believes in me shall never die" (*John* 11:23-26). As we saw in *Dying to Live,* everyone will experience life after death, not only those who believe in Jesus Christ.

This book is intended to help you prepare for the magnificent life that awaits you on the other side. And, before that, for the judgment, the final exam we must all pass in order to get there. Even if you are still not one hundred percent certain there is life after death, it is worthwhile living as if there is. You have everything to gain and nothing to lose.

What is more, as we saw in *Dying to Live,* many of the thousands of people who have had near-death experiences, people of all beliefs and of none, have experienced the judgment. The doctors who have studied these experiences call this judgment the life review. The experience of these people is uncannily similar. They see their whole life played out before their eyes as if in a movie, both the good they have done and the bad. And they are often allowed to feel what another person felt when they did something good or bad to them.

What is more, they realise that what they are seeing is the truth. If, when they did something wrong, they justified it with some excuse which seemed perfectly reasonable at the time, now in the judgment they are aware that there is no room for excuses. What they have done is done and there is no going back on it. They lived their life once and for all, and now they are examined on it. They must take the consequences for their actions.

And there is no possibility of appeal to a higher authority. They can't argue their case in the hope of having the initial judgment overturned. They are fully aware that what they are seeing is the final judgment on their life, and they accept it, for better or worse. This too, is quite extraordinary. Even those who found themselves going to hell accepted that they deserved it. They didn't think that God's judgment was unjust. They knew it was right.

The judge, as we know, is God himself, and he desperately wants everyone to pass and be with him forever. As we have seen, he is infinitely kind and merciful. We couldn't have a more compassionate judge. But he can only judge on the basis of what we give him, on the basis of our life as we have lived it. We can only live our life once. We can't go back and change anything we have done. It is important, therefore, to live this one life well, at least from now on.

The judgment is truly the final exam, the last one we will ever take. And by far the most important. It determines our fate for all eternity. Really, we have been preparing for this exam all our life, especially from the time we acquired the use of reason, around the age of six or seven, and we became responsible for our actions. A good way to understand this is that with everything we do, or don't do, we are writing another page in the book of our life. We write the last word in the moment of our death. It is this book that we will see and that God will judge in the judgment.

The purpose of the book you are now reading is to help you prepare well for that exam. You might be nearing the end of your life right now and so have little time left. But even then, you have ample time to turn a possible failure into a brilliant success, especially by being truly sorry for your sins, your offences against God and others.

Or maybe you are still young and have plenty of time to prepare. Or so you think. We can never know when we are going to die. We all know young people who have died suddenly in an accident, from a heart attack, a stroke or a burst aneurism… None of us can say how long we will live. And when we die it is too late to change anything. So, we should take life seriously and prepare well all our life. Then there will be no surprises in the final exam.

When people look at their life as it is at present, there can be two attitudes at opposite ends of the spectrum which are equally foolish and unrealistic. On one hand, there are those who look at what they have done and say: "It's too late. My life has been a disaster. I have committed every sin in the book. There is no hope for me." That is foolish and unrealistic. Everyone can change, no matter how little time they have left. God is good and he will give them all the help they need. On the other hand, there are those who know their life has not been very good but they trust in the mercy of God and make no effort to change for the better. This is equally foolish and unrealistic. God is merciful but he is also just. He wants us to change and he gives us all the help we need to do that. As they say, God helps those who help themselves.

Hopefully, you are not one of those two types, but rather someone who realises that you can change for the better and that God will help you do it. This book will help you. It will show you the path and give you hope that you can be the better person you want to be, so that when you face God, you can do so with confidence.

But, you might ask, on what basis is God going to judge me? Will it be on how I see myself, my life and my actions, in such a way that my own personal, subjective, judgment will be the standard? That would be nice. Or perhaps on how others see me? That might not be so nice. Or will it be rather according to some other standard that I don't know, like some standard that God himself sets, which will at least be fair. If so, what is that standard? I would really like to know so that I can start preparing for it. That is the topic of our next chapter.

2

Objective morality

In today's world, we see two opposed visions of morality. On one hand there are those who say that the question of morality, of what is right and wrong, is completely subjective. It is relative to how you see it personally. If you think some course of action is right and good, it is – at least for you. If someone else thinks that course of action is wrong, he is entitled to his opinion too. To each, his own. Morality is what you make of it. This is what we call moral relativism.

On the other hand, there are those who say no, that morality is objective, the same for everyone. Independently of how you see it, certain actions are in themselves simply wrong and not to be carried out, and others are right and good.

How are we to resolve this question? Or maybe we don't need to resolve it. We can simply adopt whichever approach we think best. As free human beings we can, of course, think whatever we want. We can have different opinions. And we can live our lives in accordance with our beliefs. Fine. But when we come before God in the judgment, it may be – and it is! – that he will judge us according to some objective standard which is the same for all.

When we think about it, we would probably hope and expect that that would be the case. It just doesn't seem right that, if we have made an effort all our life to refrain from doing what we knew was wrong, like being dishonest or greedy, and we struggled and sacrificed to do what was right, we would receive the same judgment and reward as someone who did whatever he pleased, including things we considered to be very wrong. This, we think, would simply not be fair. But God is fair. Thank God for that.

Or, looking at it in another way, if someone thinks it is quite okay to steal my outdoor furniture or my car, or to sleep with my wife, I would not say he is entitled to his opinion – to each his own. No, after all, some things are just plain wrong, no matter what some people may think. There must then be some objective standard of morality on which God will judge us all at the end of our life. But what could that standard be?

Ancient philosophers like Aristotle, who lived in the fourth century before Christ, Cicero, who followed him three centuries later, and many others found the objective standard of morality in human nature. The word nature, by the way, refers to what makes something to be what it is and not something else. So trees have tree nature, horses have horse nature and humans have human nature. Given that all human beings, by definition, have human nature, that nature provides a standard of morality which is common to all. That standard is the natural law.

Those who might be inclined to reject the idea of natural law out of hand should consider three concepts that most people accept without question, and which presuppose the existence of a natural law. They are the concepts of *human rights*, *natural justice* and *crimes against humanity*.

Human rights

Everyone admits that people have human rights, rights which they have, not because their government grants them, but because they have from the mere fact of being human. For example, we have the right to life, so it should be a crime to kill an innocent human being. Or the right to freedom of speech, so that we will not be put in jail for disagreeing with government policy. Or the right to live and work wherever we want, to marry and raise a family, etc.

These rights are prior to human laws, not based on human laws. Historically, man had human rights from the very moment he appeared on earth, and it was only much later that he established a system of human laws to protect those rights. Human rights are inherent in human nature itself.

A good number of human rights are enshrined in the United Nations Universal Declaration of Human Rights in 1948. For example, Article 1 of the Declaration states: "All human beings are born free and equal in dignity and rights."

The Declaration does not say that only human beings in the countries which are signatories of the Declaration are equal in dignity and rights, but rather "all human beings." Nor does it say that the Declaration is granting them this dignity and these rights. Rather, they are *"born* ... equal in dignity and rights." They have that dignity and those rights by the very fact of being born as human beings. The Declaration is thus acknowledging a set of rights which are prior to and independent of human laws. Human rights are based on human nature itself.

Natural Justice

Another concept that people readily accept is that of natural justice. For example, if the legislature in a given country, or a dictator for that matter, passed a law which allowed a person to be put in jail and held without charge for ten years, we would all object that the law was a violation of natural justice. Or if the law provided for all people to be killed at government expense when they turned sixty-five in order to save money for the state, again we would protest that that was a violation of natural justice. It was an unjust law. When we speak of natural justice or an unjust law, by what standard are we measuring it? We are in effect saying that there is a higher law than state law, a law based on human nature, to which state law should be conformed. This is the natural law.

Crimes against humanity

Right-minded people agree that there are certain crimes which a particular country might carry out with the authority of their leaders which are so fundamentally wrong that they are crimes against humanity. For example, history has given us examples of genocide, the effort to eliminate all people of a particular race, the imprisonment and killing of people of a particular religion or of people who are mentally handicapped, the indiscriminate killing of innocent civilians in a war, and so on. Again, there must be a higher standard by which such crimes can be measured and condemned as crimes against humanity. It is the natural law.

The natural law

Coming back to what the natural law is, in simple terms it can be defined as the series of rights and duties deriving from human nature. Obviously, in this context we are referring to the natural *moral* law, which establishes rights and duties, or rights and wrongs, by which human conduct is to be guided.

That is, they are rights and duties which are derived not from human legislation, such as the right to drive a car or to vote at a certain age, but rather from human nature itself. In other words, for the fact that someone is a human person he has a series of rights and duties that are inherent in his nature, rights and duties that are therefore prior to human legislation.

Looking at it in another way, they are rights and duties written in human nature itself, much as the law of gravity is written in the nature of physical bodies. For example, scientists can study physical nature and discover laws written in it – the laws of physics, chemistry, thermodynamics, etc. – that describe how the body will behave under certain conditions and how to treat it so as not to destroy it.

So too, we can study human nature and discover in it ethical laws, rights and duties, principles of right and wrong, that describe how man ought to act if he wants to achieve the maximum of human flourishing and how he ought not to act if he wants to avoid harming himself and others. That is, there are principles of morality inherent in human nature.

For example, it is obvious that if people were allowed to steal others' property whenever they wanted, no one would feel safe and society could not function. Or if it were permissible to kill an innocent human being, again we would not feel safe and society could not function. There are certain forms of conduct which are simply wrong, contrary to human nature and to the flourishing of individuals and society.

We would all agree with that. If someone asked you under what circumstances it would be acceptable for him to kill your daughter, you would be outraged by the mere question. Or under what circumstances he could burn down your house, you would shudder. That is, there are certain forms of conduct which are simply wrong, and always wrong, because they are contrary to human nature. They are what we call moral absolutes.

In other words, there is an objective standard of morality, based on human nature, which we call the natural law. It is by this objective standard that God will judge us. This is fair, since all human beings of whatever country, race, field of work, or period of history for that matter, share a common nature and therefore they can be judged by the same standard.

The French philosopher Jacques Maritain, in a 1942 book entitled *The Rights of Man and Natural Law*, put it this way:

> Since I have not space here to discuss nonsense (you can always find very intelligent philosophers to defend it most brilliantly), I am taking it for granted that you admit that there is a human nature

and that this human nature is the same in all men. I am taking it for granted that you also admit that man is a being gifted with intelligence, and who, as such, acts with an understanding of what he is doing, and therefore with the power to determine for himself the ends which he pursues. On the other hand, possessed of a nature, being constituted in a given, determinate fashion, man obviously possesses ends which correspond to his natural constitution and which are the same for all – as all pianos, for instance, whatever their particular type and in whatever spot they may be, have as their end the production of certain attuned sounds. If they don't produce these sounds they must be tuned or discarded as worthless. But since man is endowed with intelligence and determines his own ends, it is up to him to put himself in tune with the ends necessarily demanded by his nature. This means that there is, by very virtue of human nature, an order or a disposition which human reason can discover and according to which the human will must act in order to attune itself to the necessary ends of the human being. The unwritten law, or natural law, is nothing more than that (*The Rights of Man and Natural Law,* Ignatius Press, San Francisco 1986, pp. 140-141).

This couldn't be clearer. Man has a certain nature which is common to all human beings and if he wants to find the well-being and happiness he seeks, he must attune himself, adjust his behaviour, to that nature, avoiding whatever is contrary to it and doing what is consistent with it.

The natural law, by the way, is called natural for two reasons: it derives from human nature, and it can be known by natural means, by reasoned reflection on human nature. The natural law has certain characteristics.

Characteristics of the natural law

First, the natural law is originally *unwritten*. It is, as we have seen, a set of ethical principles, rights and duties, which can be derived from a consideration of human nature. Over time philosophers, ethicists and theologians have elaborated the essential content of the natural law and written it down. Of course, in any age there may be disagreement about certain secondary precepts of it. But the fact that some individuals or peoples may not have accepted some of those precepts says nothing against the validity of the natural law itself, any more than the fact that someone may misunderstand a principle of mathematics says anything against the validity of mathematics.

Second, the natural law is *universal*. That is, it applies to all beings possessed of human nature. There is not one natural law for Europeans and another for Africans or Asians, since all human beings have the same nature. Following from the human nature common to all, all persons have the same fundamental rights and duties.

Third, the natural law is *immutable*, unchanging, just as human nature is immutable. Man has the same nature today as he did at the dawn of civilisation. Evidence of this is the continuing appeal of the ancient writings of Greek playwrights or of the Old Testament of the Bible or of Shakespeare, which speak about human beings with the same characteristics as we have today. Naturally we now live and travel and communicate in a more technologically advanced way than our forebears, but our human nature has not changed. Just as it was wrong for Cain to kill his brother Abel, as narrated in the first book of the Old Testament, it is wrong today. And it will always be wrong.

Fourth, the natural law *cannot be abolished*. Just as physical laws, such as the law of gravity cannot be abolished – they are simply part of the nature of things – , or the laws of health cannot be abolished – if you drink alcohol to excess your judgment will be impaired, you will feel sick and eventually you may suffer liver disease – so the natural moral law cannot be abolished. It is written in human nature itself. Or, more simply, human nature cannot be abolished.

As a consequence, if a person, even though unaware of the precepts of the natural law, violates some precept, he and possibly others will suffer in some way. For example, if someone habitually lies, others will be deceived and possibly hurt, and they will soon realise this and will not trust him in anything he says. That is, when the natural law is observed there is a certain flourishing in human society, and when it is not observed there is a certain disruption.

The natural law in the ancient world

Is the concept of natural law a Christian invention? Certainly not. It is much older than Christianity.

If someone wants an ancient example of the awareness of the natural law as more powerful than human law, he can find it in the thirteenth century BC in the book of Exodus of the Bible. When the king of Egypt ordered midwives attending the Hebrew women to kill any male children they delivered, two of them realised that this was wrong and they refused to obey the king (cf. *Exodus* 1:15-21).

In the East there is evidence of the idea of a universal law binding on man in Oriental literature, such as that of China, long before the rise of philosophy in the West.

But the origin of a natural law doctrine, with its elaboration as an unbroken, continuous development, is first to be found among the ancient Greek poets and historians. Sophocles (c. 497-406 BC), Thucydides (c. 460-400 BC), and Zenophon (c. 427-355 BC) all presented a concept of the natural law that is divine, universal, and known to all.

The Greek philosophers, using observation and experience, saw an order in the universe associated with a predictable, regular recurrence of events which they attributed to an ordering principle or law that rules the cosmos. They saw human beings too, as part of the cosmos, as subject to that ordering law, which in their case is the right or the just by nature. Morals and human law, for the Greeks, thus have their foundation in the harmony of nature or the natural law. This law exists independently of human will and has universal validity. It provides objective principles and ideals to which human beings must conform, by their very nature.

Sophocles

An eloquent example is the Greek playwright Sophocles. In his *Antigone*, first performed in 441 BC, Sophocles recognises that human laws are subject to a higher divine law. Antigone was condemned to be buried alive for burying the body of her brother Polyneices, thus violating the order of Creon, king of Thebes, who had decreed that Polyneices' corpse was to be left exposed and that no Theban was to bury or mourn him. The following dialogue ensues between Creon and Antigone:

> "*Creon:* Now tell me, briefly and concisely: were you aware of the proclamation prohibiting those acts?
>
> *Antigone:* I was. I couldn't avoid it when it was made public.
>
> *Creon:* You still dared break this law?
>
> *Antigone:* Yes, because I did not believe that Zeus was the one who had proclaimed it; neither did Justice, or the gods of the dead whom Justice lives among. The laws they have made for men are well marked out. I didn't suppose your decree had strength enough for you, who are human, to violate the lawful traditions the gods have not written merely, but made infallible. These laws are not for now or for yesterday, they are alive forever; and no one knows when they were shown to us first. I did not intend to pay, before the gods, for breaking these laws because of my fear of one man and his principles. I was thoroughly aware I would die before you proclaimed it; of course I would die, even if you hadn't. Since I will die, and early, I call this profit. Anyone who lives the troubled life I do must benefit from death.
>
> "No, I do not suffer from the fact of death. But if I had let my own brother stay unburied I would have suffered all the pain I do not

feel now. And if you decide what I did was foolish, you may be fool enough to convict me too."

Antigone is saying, in essence, that there is a natural duty to bury one's own brother and no human law can stand in the way of that duty. It is better to follow the natural law and be punished for it by man, than to follow the law of man and be punished for it by God.

Aristotle

A century later, the Greek philosopher Aristotle (384-322 BC), in his *Nicomachean Ethics*, made the distinction between natural justice and legal justice, or in our terms between natural law and human law:

> What is just in the political sense can be subdivided into what is just by nature and what is just by convention. What is by nature just has the same force everywhere and does not depend on what we regard or do not regard as just. In what is just by convention, on the other hand, it makes originally no difference whether it is fixed one way or another, but it does make a difference once it is fixed, for example, that a prisoner's ransom shall be one mina...
> (*Nicomachean Ethics*, Book 5).

Elsewhere Aristotle writes that "there is in nature a common principle of the just and unjust that all people in some way divine, even if they have no association or commerce with each other" (*On Rhetoric*, Book I, Chap. 13).

What Aristotle says about all people being able to discern what is just and unjust is borne out by the fact that the early Romans, as they extended their empire to all the peoples around the Mediterranean as well as to Germany and Britain, discovered in the different civilisations some common moral and legal principles which they codified as the *Ius gentium*, the law of the nations or the law of foreigners. They saw in this common denominator of moral and legal principles a law of nature which was common to all peoples.

This is only to be expected. Even today, all countries have laws forbidding and punishing theft, murder and so on. It is because such acts are naturally wrong, a violation of natural justice, that all countries forbid and punish them.

Cicero

Turning now to Rome, Cicero (106-43 BC) played an important role in developing the idea of natural law. He described law, or the natural law, as "the highest reason, implanted in Nature, which commands what ought to be done and forbids the opposite" (*Laws*). This law, he taught, precedes written human law and the state and embodies basic principles of justice and right conduct.

Following Aristotle's distinction between natural law and human law and ridiculing the idea, current in his day, that the only law was human law, Cicero writes:

> Socrates was right when he cursed, as he often did, the man who first separated utility from Justice; for this separation, he complained, is the source of all mischief... But the most foolish notion of all is the belief that everything is just which is found in the customs or laws of nations... But if the principles of Justice were founded on the decrees of people, the edicts of princes, or the decisions of judges, then Justice would sanction robbery and adultery and forgery of wills, in case these acts were approved by the votes or decrees of the populace (*Laws*).

That is, Cicero is saying that even though a human law were to approve of robbery or forgery, that law would still be unjust, because it is contrary to the natural law. It would be a case of an unjust law. Elsewhere in that same work, Cicero writes:

> What is right and true is also eternal, and does not begin or end with written statutes... From this point of view it can be readily understood that those who formulated wicked and unjust statutes for nations, thereby breaking their promises and agreements, put into effect anything but "laws". It may thus be clear that in the very definition of the term "law" there inheres the idea and principle of choosing what is just and true... Therefore Law is

the distinction between things just and unjust, made in agreement with that primal and most ancient of all things, Nature; and in conformity to nature's standard are framed those human laws which inflict punishment upon the wicked but defend and protect the good (*Laws*).

Again, Cicero is saying that there is a higher standard, that of nature or natural justice, by which human laws can be judged to be just or unjust. This higher standard is the natural law, which is as ancient and eternal as human nature itself.

How does one come to know the natural law? Cicero answers that it is through reason; that is, by using one's intellect to reflect on human nature. He even goes so far as to equate the natural law with right reason: "True law is right reason in accord with nature" (*Republic*. III, 22, 33).

In a magnificent statement, Cicero affirms the universality, immutability and binding force of the natural law:

> Changeless and everlasting, it imbues all men. By its commands it summons to duty, by its prohibitions it averts from wrongdoing... To alter this law, or to repeal any part of it, is forbidden by all that is holy, while to abolish it is impossible. We can be freed from it neither by the senate nor by the people, nor need we look outside ourselves for its expounder or interpreter. Nor will there be one law in Rome and another at Athens, one now and another in ages to come. Rather a single sempiternal and immutable law will hold among all nations for all time. And there will be one master and commander over us all, God the author, promulgator, and enforcing judge of this law (*Republic, III, 22, 33*).

By the end of the classical age of Roman jurisprudence in the third century AD, hundreds of texts had referred to *ius naturale, naturalis ratio,* and *rerum natura* (natural law, natural reason, the nature of things). Thus, the great Roman jurist Ulpian, who died in 228, could state that, insofar as the *ius civile* or human law was concerned, slaves were not regarded as persons, but under the natural law all men were equal (*Digest* 50.17.32).

Human laws and the natural law

It is not only individuals who should rule their lives by the natural law. Countries too should pass laws in conformity with it. The role of human law is to determine further for a particular society the practical details of the precepts of the natural law. For example, in further determining the natural right to private property, human law determines particular forms of ownership and transfer of property and punishments for stealing another's goods. The right to life is protected by laws defining and punishing different forms of killing, such as manslaughter, murder, etc., and by laws regarding the possession and use of firearms. Human law is necessary in any society. Hence the adage *ubi societas, ibi ius*, where there is a society, there is law.

If the laws of a country contradict the natural law, they are *ipso facto* invalid and unjust. Thomas Aquinas, the brilliant thirteenth-century theologian and philosopher, goes so far as to call such a law an act of violence:

> Human law has the nature of law insofar as it partakes of right reason; and it is clear that, in this respect, it is derived from the eternal law. But insofar as it deviates from reason, it is called an unjust law, and has the nature, not of law but of violence (*Summa Theologiae*, I-II, q. 93, art. 3).

Martin Luther King, in his "Letter from Birmingham Jail" in 1963, echoed these thoughts of Aquinas and quoted him:

> A just law is a man-made code that squares with the moral law or the law of God... An unjust law is a code that is out of harmony with the moral law. To put it in the terms of Saint Thomas Aquinas: "An unjust law is a human law that is not rooted in eternal law and natural law."

This principle was seen too in the Nuremberg trials after the Second World War, when the courts found certain laws passed by the Nazis to be in contradiction with the natural law and therefore unjust. For example, one court rejected the defence of accused physicians that their killing of prisoners in medical experiments had been authorised by the laws of the Third Reich. The court stated: "Law must be defined as an ordinance or precept devised in the service of justice. Whenever the conflict between an enacted law and true justice reaches unendurable proportions, the enacted law must yield to justice, and be considered a 'lawless law.' The accused may not justify his conduct by appealing to an existing law if this law offended against certain self-evident principles of the natural law" (*Suddeutsche Juristen Zeitschrift* 521 (1947)).

Thus, the natural law constitutes a higher norm, an objective standard, by which human laws can be judged to be just or unjust. Human laws are particularly unjust when they not only permit conduct contrary to the natural law, but actually command it. For example, if the law allows the killing of the most innocent of human beings, the unborn child, by abortion, a person can simply choose not to have an abortion. But if the law were to require an abortion where, for example, a couple already had two children, it would be especially iniquitous and could not be obeyed. It would be a particularly unjust law.

Moral absolutes

From all of this it is clear that there is an objective foundation for morality, applicable to all human beings. That foundation is human nature, which we all have in common. On the basis of the precepts of the natural law, God can judge all of us by the same standard. In other words, morality is not subjective, dependent on how each individual sees it, but objective, based on a common standard.

This gives us what we call moral absolutes, certain forms of conduct that are always right or always wrong. In simple terms, conduct that is ordered to the good of the human person is right, and conduct that is contrary to that good is wrong. On this basis, some acts are intrinsically evil, or wrong, no matter what the intention of the person doing them, or the circumstances.

Deep down, we can see the truth of this. There are actions like rape, killing an innocent person and stealing another's property that are simply wrong in themselves. They are intrinsically evil. They go against the good of the human person and of the stability of society. It doesn't make any difference what reasons a person had for doing these things, or the circumstances in which they did them. The actions are wrong in themselves.

All countries have laws punishing these forms of behaviour, and we are all grateful for that. It gives us a greater sense of security and peace. If in the laws of a country everything were a matter of "do whatever you think best under the circumstances", who would protect us from a neighbour who judged it quite acceptable to steal our car, burn down our house or rape our teenage daughter? Granted, these crimes are being committed now, but there would be no end to them if the laws of the country did not forbid them and punish them. Moral chaos would reign.

So no, morality is not a matter of what each person thinks it is. It is not subjective. It is objective. On that basis God will judge all of us by the same standard. If you want to live the rest of your life well so as to be better prepared for the final exam when you die, what must you do in more particular terms? We will study that in the following chapters, but first some general considerations.

Thomas Aquinas derives the morality of particular acts by examining the natural inclinations of human beings. He writes: "All those things to which man has a natural inclination, are naturally apprehended by reason as being good, and consequently as objects of pursuit, and their contraries as evil, and objects of avoidance" (*Summa Theologiae*, I-II, q. 94, art. 2).

Let us follow this line of reasoning and see what we can deduce about the morality of particular acts. I must warn you that what follows is my own reasoning, not that of St Thomas, although it follows from his premise.

We see, for example, that humans have a natural inclination to believe in a supreme being of some sort and to worship that being. From this inclination comes the duty and right to worship God according to one's own conscience. Human law, at least in democratic countries, protects this right by allowing freedom of worship.

Humans have a natural inclination to marry and form a family. From this comes the right to marry and the duty to look after one's spouse and children. Human law protects the institution of marriage and establishes norms for the validity of marriage and procedures to follow should the marriage break up. It also punishes child abuse and child neglect.

Humans have a natural inclination to live together with others in society, which in turn requires some form of government of that society. This involves rights such as that of expressing one's views to those in government and duties such as obeying just laws and paying taxes.

Humans have a natural inclination to preserve their life. This gives rise to the most basic of all rights, the right to life, as well as to the right to sufficient food and shelter, and to duties such as those of not killing others, not endangering their life unnecessarily, etc. Human laws regulate these rights and duties through the prohibition and punishment of murder, manslaughter, assault, driving a vehicle under the influence of alcohol, etc.

Humans have a natural inclination to own property in order to house and support their family with some sense of security. It gives rise to the right to own property and the duty not to steal or damage that of others, all of which are regulated by human law.

Humans have a natural inclination to communicate their ideas and feelings to others and for this they have the gift of speech, which involves the duty to tell the truth and the right to hear the truth as well as the right to a good name. These too are regulated by human laws regarding fraud, perjury, defamation, slander, etc.

As you can see, it is not difficult to reflect on human nature and derive very quickly a series of rights and duties, rights and wrongs, based on that nature. They are rights and duties that constitute particular precepts of the natural law. They are accepted by all democratic countries and are enshrined in their laws. Naturally, what we have just seen is only a bare outline of some of the more basic precepts of the natural law. We will see these precepts in greater detail in the following chapters.

It must be remembered of course that not all the inclinations which we feel as natural are in fact truly an expression of human nature as such. Some inclinations, such as the inclination to eat or drink to excess, to be lazy and avoid work or to be selfish, are disordered inclinations which have resulted from what theologians call original sin, or human weakness. It is only the truly natural inclinations that give rise to the rights and duties we call the natural law.

Before we look at particular precepts of the natural law we need to lay the foundations of our moral life in general. We need to study such topics as whether we are really free to make choices at all, the role conscience plays in our decisions, the importance of our emotions, the different types of sin, etc. That is the topic of the next chapter.

3

Foundations of moral life

Human freedom

The first aspect of moral life, the foundation, as it were, of our actions, is human freedom. Whether we pass the final exam or not depends on our being truly free and responsible, able to weigh up the consequences of our possible courses of action and then decide freely which to choose.

But are we really free? Most people readily accept that of course we are. After all, we are conscious of being free, of being able to choose one course of action or another. That we are not determined by our genes, or the neurons in our brain for that matter, to do this or that. What is more, we know that when we do something good and generous, we have a sense of satisfaction, because we freely chose to do it and it cost us some effort. Or when we have done the wrong thing, we have a sense of guilt, because we could very well not have done it. All of this is telling us that we are truly free, and responsible, for our actions. This is the common experience of everyone.

Of course there are some people, a tiny minority to be sure, who deny that we are free. They say that, in one way or another, we are determined to act in a particular way. We are conditioned, they say, by the neurons in our brain, by our biology or the environment in which we grew up and now live...

Even though certain individuals may deny the reality of human freedom, the legal system of countries does not. If someone has been found guilty of a crime, that person is punished. The judge does not say, "You have been found guilty of stealing, but I know you couldn't help it because you were determined to steal by the chemical processes in your brain, or your deprived upbringing, so I won't have you punished." Similarly, many countries grant awards for bravery or heroism, and other honours to people who have done significant deeds in the service of society. They do this because they recognise that the recipients were free to do what they did or not to do it, and they reward them because they did it. Parents too acknowledge the freedom of their children, punishing them for their misdeeds and rewarding them for their good ones.

In our freedom we are radically different from animals, even the highest ones. We have a rational intellect and a free will and we are capable of weighing up the various courses of action before us and then deciding freely what to do. Animals cannot do this. They only follow their instincts. As evidence of our rational intelligence, we humans are constantly making progress in so many fields – communication, transportation, medicine, etc. – whereas even the highest animals continue to live in the same way they always have.

What do we mean by freedom? Freedom can be defined as the power, rooted in intellect and will, to act or not to act, to do this or that, and so to perform deliberate actions on our own responsibility. That is, free will involves the power to choose: to act or not to act, to follow one course of action or another. And because the person has deliberately chosen a course of action from among various possibilities, he or she is responsible for that choice.

Responsibility necessarily goes with freedom. If we misuse our freedom in human affairs we have to answer to our family, to our employer or the government, and it is the same before God. If we choose rightly and do what God is asking of us, we find happiness and God will reward us both in this life and in the next. And if we go against God's law, we will suffer the consequences. Christ himself spoke of the reward to be given to those who have been faithful: "Well done, good and faithful servant; you have been faithful over a little, I will set you over much; enter into the joy of your master" (*Matthew* 25:23).

What is more, in some way our free choices shape our life. They can make us progressively a better person – a more kind, hardworking, honest one – or alternatively a more lazy, self-centred, dishonest one. St Gregory of Nyssa, a fourth century bishop, expresses the same idea. He says that "we are in a certain way our own parents, creating ourselves as we will, by our decisions" (*De vita Moysis*, II, 2-3).

We can all identify with this. The more we use our freedom wisely, the more we shape our life for the better. The more we work hard, day after day, the more we form the habit of doing so, and the easier it becomes. The more we refrain from having that extra drink, the stronger we become in living sobriety. What is more, the more we do what is good, the freer we become. Why is this? Because, when all is said and done, the only freedom that matters is the freedom to live a good life, to be that better, happy person we all want to be. So the more we make it easier to do the right thing by actually doing it, the freer we are. Similarly, the more we make the wrong choices, the more we become, in a sense, slaves of our passions.

We see this clearly in the many people who have become slaves to various addictions – alcohol, gambling, pornography, etc. They would be the first ones to tell us they are no longer free. I think, for example, of that young man who had given up the use of recreational drugs and went to a party where they were freely available. When a girl offered him a marijuana cigarette, he said no, prompting her reply: "I wish I could say no."

So, we want to use our freedom wisely, to make good choices and shape ourselves for the better. We desperately want to pass that final exam.

Conscience

If there is one topic about which there is a great deal of confusion these days it is the role of conscience. What is conscience? We all have a general notion of conscience as an inner voice that tells us what is right and wrong. It is traditionally defined as a judgment of the mind whereby the human person recognises the moral quality of a concrete act that he is going to perform, is in the process of performing, or has already completed.

Looking closely at the definition, we see that conscience is first of all a judgment of our mind. It is not a feeling or an intuition. It is a judgment. Also, it is a judgment about the morality of a concrete, particular act that the person is considering doing, is carrying out or has done in the past. It is not the role of conscience to judge the morality of acts in general, such as lying, stealing, killing the innocent, etc. That role belongs to our intellect in learning about morality, as you are doing now in reading this book. Rather, it is the role of conscience to apply what we know about morality in general to a particular act, telling us whether the act is right or wrong. And, as the definition makes clear, conscience has a role to play in judging the morality of acts we have done in the past, so that we may feel guilty or happy about acts done days or even years before.

The important question is, on what basis does conscience make this judgment? The answer is obvious. It judges on the basis of what we have previously learned about morality. Consider another type of judgment some people will make. If they want to make a wise investment of some money they have inherited, they will do it on the basis of what they have learned about the risks and potential returns of various forms of investment. And they may also ask the advice of financial planners. So too, with conscience we make judgments on the basis of what we have learned about right and wrong, and if we are uncertain, we can consult someone who knows. Except that our moral choices are much more important than our financial ones. Here it is not a matter of making or losing some money, but of making or losing our immortal soul, and with it our happiness for all eternity.

So conscience is not a law unto itself. Rather it looks to the law of God and applies that law to the particular act we are considering doing. In this sense it may be likened to a sextant, which sailors formerly used to know where they were by looking at a fixed point of reference in the stars and other heavenly bodies. Without the stars, the sextant is useless. Without the fixed point of reference of the law of God, conscience is blind.

This implies the important duty of forming our conscience well: of learning what is right and wrong, in accordance with the objective standard we considered in the last chapter. The objective standard, of course, is the natural law, the law of God. We will study this in depth in the following chapters. Only when we have a well-formed conscience can we make judgements in conformity with the true good of the human person.

But even when we have a good idea of what is right and wrong, we can still face another difficulty. That is the temptation to push our conscience into the background, not to listen to it, especially when we are strongly inclined to do something we know to be wrong. It might be because we want to have a few more drinks, look at pornography, steal something from a shop, or whatever. We all face this situation from time to time. When we are tempted to do the wrong thing, we will always find it easier to prefer our own inclinations to the voice of our conscience. But we should be honest and courageous enough to listen to what our conscience is telling us and then follow it. That is the way we will do what is right, be happy with what we have done, and deserve to pass the final exam.

Are we obliged to follow our conscience? Yes, whenever our conscience is certain, that is, not doubtful, and it is commanding or forbidding us to do something. To act against our conscience in that situation would be to do wrong, to commit sin, since we would be acting against what we knew to be the law of God. If on the other hand our conscience is doubtful, not certain, and we are unsure of whether the act is right or wrong, we should make every effort to resolve the doubt by asking someone whose judgment we trust, or by reading a book which answers our question. If we have to act immediately, and there is no time to consult someone, we can choose what we perceive to be the safer course. We desperately want to pass the final exam and, as with exams we have taken in this life, if we are unsure of something that may be on the exam, we make an effort to find the answer before we take the exam.

Virtues and vices

Some of the exams we take here on earth test our knowledge of a particular subject, and others involve demonstrating that we have the skill to carry out particular tasks. Among the latter, for example, are a piano exam, which tests our ability to play certain pieces to a certain standard, a driving exam, which tests our ability to drive a car safely, and a carpentry exam, which tests our skill in performing the required tasks.

In order to pass those practical exams we practise the particular discipline over and over so that we are truly proficient in it. The more we practise, the better we become at doing it. Through practice, we form a habit and the habit facilitates doing the task.

The final exam at the end of our life is a practical one. God is not going to ask us how much we knew about him or about his law, but rather how much we loved him and did his will. And then, when in the course of our life we failed to do what was right, as of course we often will, he will ask us whether we were truly sorry and resolved to try harder in the future.

Just as our practice of the piano, of driving, or of woodworking helped us form good habits in those disciplines, so our practice of good deeds of charity, hard work and honesty help us form good habits to make us a better person. These good habits in our moral life are called virtues. They are simply good habits that facilitate the doing of good acts. The more we do these acts the more we form the corresponding good habits, and the easier it is to do the right thing.

But let's be honest. We can also find it easy, and perhaps even easier, to form bad habits, which we call vices. We can get into the habit of eating too much, drinking too much alcohol, being lazy, watching too much television, being selfish and uncaring, etc. Then the vices can predominate and we find it harder to do the good deeds we want to do. So, life involves a struggle to do what is right and form the virtues we need in order to be the person we want to be, and to avoid doing the wrong thing and forming the corresponding vices.

Which are some of the most important good habits, or virtues? Three very important ones, which refer to our relationship with God as well as with our fellow man, are faith, hope and love.

By faith, we believe in God and in anything we have not seen. For example, practically all we know, we know by faith. What we know about the geography, government and history of countries we have not visited we know by faith, believing what the teachers and textbooks tell us. The same applies to our knowledge of science and so many other disciplines. We believe what we read in books, in what others say, and in what the newspapers tell us, even though some of these may be mistaken. How much more sensible it is, then, to believe what God tells us about himself, about life after death, etc. This is the virtue of faith. Whenever we are tempted not to believe something that we know to be true, we can practise the virtue of faith by assenting to it on the basis that the person teaching it is worthy of our trust.

Hope is sometimes defined as the firm expectation of a difficult good not yet possessed. It inclines us to trust that a difficult good can be achieved. This can be a human good like finding a job, overcoming an illness, winning a game, or even that the weather will improve for our picnic. Or it can be a spiritual good like becoming a better person and going to heaven when we die. Again, when we are inclined to become discouraged and despair that we can achieve some good, we can move ourselves to hope that, especially with the help of God who loves us and is all powerful, we can make it a reality.

Charity, or love, is the virtue that facilitates loving God, who is all good and worthy of our love, and also loving our neighbour, understood as all those around us. The more we practise loving God through our prayer and worship of him, and the more we put ourselves out for those around us, the easier it becomes and so we grow in charity, we please God and we prepare for the judgment.

The ancient philosophers like Aristotle also distinguished four human virtues which they considered to be of special importance: prudence, justice, fortitude and temperance. These virtues are also mentioned in the Bible in the book of Wisdom (cf. *Wisdom* 8:7).

Prudence is often defined as the virtue that helps us discern our true good and to choose the best way of achieving it. This virtue is fundamental. It helps us determine what is most important in our life, to set our priorities, so that we do not waste time pursuing what is of less importance. It is a sorry person indeed who does not know what is truly good for him or her, or has not chosen the best way of achieving it. We can grow in prudence by investigating thoroughly the facts of the situation, evaluating the pros and cons of the possible courses of action, thinking the matter through carefully before we act, consulting others when we are doubtful, and then carrying out our decision with confidence.

Justice is traditionally defined as the virtue which helps us give to each one what is due to him. This can be to give to God what is due to him, such as our love and worship, and also to give to our neighbour what is owed to him in justice. By living justice, we respect our neighbour's rights, we are fair in all our dealings, we pay our lawful debts, we honour the terms of contracts, and so on. It is a fundamental virtue for harmony and stability in society.

Fortitude, or will power, is the virtue that ensures firmness in difficulties and constancy in the pursuit of the good. It is sometimes called courage. Again, we can see how important it is, especially when we lack will power to do something we know we should do, or we readily give in to the temptation to do the wrong thing. We can grow in fortitude by doing whatever we find hard: getting out of bed on time in the morning, striving to overcome laziness and softness, working hard and finishing a task, giving ourselves to our family when we are tired, etc. Fortitude can be likened to the spurs that the rider uses to urge the horse on to continue running hard until the end of the race.

Temperance is the virtue that moderates the search for pleasure and provides balance in the use of earthly goods. Whereas fortitude is associated with a difficult good and it strengthens the will to pursue that good, temperance is associated with a pleasurable good and it moderates the unbridled search for that pleasure. It can be likened to the reins that hold the horse back when it wants to run out of control. Temperance moderates the search for such pleasures as those of eating and drinking, sexual pleasure, and various forms of entertainment. God wants us to enjoy the pleasures of life, and for this reason he gave us the senses. But we should seek to enjoy them with moderation. We can grow in temperance by dominating our desire to seek pleasures in a disordered way.

Again, the more we practise these virtues, the easier we will find it to do what is right. Then we will prepare ourselves very well to live and die well, and to face God with confidence in the judgment.

Emotions

The emotions, or feelings, believe it or not, play an important role in our moral life. They can make it easier, or harder, to do the right thing. We all have emotions. Think of emotions like love, joy, desire, and hope, all of which relate to something good. Or anger, fear, hatred and sadness, which relate to something perceived to be bad or harmful. The emotions, sometimes called passions, are part of our nature. We all have them. In a sense, they are all good. It is understandable that we should love, desire, hope for and enjoy something good, but we should equally fear, hate, and feel angry and sad in the face of something bad. You mean we should hate? Yes, naturally we shouldn't hate persons, but we should hate the evil they do.

How do the emotions influence our acts? First, given that they are simply feelings, not acts of the will, they are neither sinful nor meritorious in themselves. Just as it is not wrong to feel hungry or cold, it is not sinful to feel angry or sad. Only when the will enters and we freely choose to do something or not to do it, do the passions influence the morality of our acts. Thus, for example, if we feel angry towards someone who has hurt us and we give in to the anger, abusing the person by our speech or our actions, we will have done wrong, even though the wrong act will be less culpable because we were moved by anger. But if we feel angry and nonetheless make an effort to treat the person well, our kindness will have all the more merit, because we had to go against the feeling of anger. Similarly, if we are threatened with harm and, as a result, we do something wrong moved by fear, that act will be less blameworthy than if we were not threatened.

The emotions can be very helpful in the moral life. For example, the deeply felt emotion of love for God makes it easier to pray and worship him. And our deeply felt love for a human person, makes it easier to show kindness and put ourselves out for them. But when the feeling of love is lacking, when we rather experience dryness and indifference, our worship of God and our acts of kindness towards a person have more merit, because they require a greater act of the will, a greater love in the true sense of willing the good of another.

As part of our moral life, we need to learn to control our emotions, especially those that relate to something evil. Some people have great difficulty controlling their anger, fear, hated for persons or sadness, and so they need to discipline themselves in this area, struggling not to give in to these emotions. Here the virtues, especially love, temperance and fortitude, are very helpful.

Sin

We have frequently used the word sin, referring to an act that is wrong, and we are all familiar with the term. But what exactly do we mean by it? A simple definition is "a wilful violation of the law of God". Following the definition, for something to be sinful, it must first be wilful, in the sense that we freely choose it, and it must also be a violation of a law of God. We will study God's law in depth in the following chapters. It is important to understand why some actions are wrong. It is not that they are wrong because God arbitrarily declared them to be so, but rather God declared them to be so because they went against the true good of man, they were harmful to man.

There are different types of sins. They can be sins of thought, word, or deed, but also sins of omission of something we should have done. For example, if we fail to come to the help of our ageing parents, that is a sin of omission.

Not all sins are equally serious. Some sins, like adultery, killing an innocent person or stealing a large sum of money are very serious, and are sometimes referred to as mortal sins. The word mortal, by the way, comes from the Latin word for death. These sins separate us from God until we repent of them, and so they are, in a sense, death-dealing to the soul. Other sins are less serious, like eating too much, telling white lies, or gossiping about others. These are sometimes called venial sins, from the Latin word meaning pardonable. Naturally, God will forgive all our sins if we are truly sorry for them. Venial sins don't separate us from God altogether, although they do wound or weaken our relationship with him. What is more, they can lead progressively to committing more serious sins. If we truly love God, as we should, we will be sorry for all of our sins.

For a sin to be mortal, it is traditionally taught that three conditions must be met. First, it must involve grave or serious matter, like adultery, murder, stealing a large sum of money, destroying another's good reputation, etc. Second there must be full knowledge not only that the act is wrong, but that it is seriously so. And third, there must be deliberate consent. If any of these conditions is lacking, the sin may be venial or no sin at all. For example, if a person knew that something was wrong but not that it was a serious sin, God would not hold the person responsible for serious sin, but probably only for a venial sin. And if the person had no idea that it was wrong at all, due to an erroneous conscience, God would not hold them responsible for any sin. Similarly, strong passion, or emotion, could reduce the deliberateness of the consent, reducing the person's guilt before God.

You have probably heard about what are called the "seven deadly sins", sometimes called the seven "capital sins". They have even been popularised in films. These principal sins, or better, vices, are pride, avarice, envy, wrath, lust, gluttony, and sloth. They are called capital, from the Latin word for head, because they easily lead to other sins. They were spoken of already in the fifth century by monks St John Cassian and St Gregory the Great.

As we saw in *Dying to Live,* if someone were to die without being sorry for a mortal sin, that person could not go to heaven. They would deprive themselves forever of the love of God and of the joy of heaven, and they would go to hell by their own free choice. They would fail the final exam. In consequence, we should do everything possible to grow in the virtues, which will make it easier to do what is right and avoid falling into sin. And we should tell God we are sorry for all our sins as soon as we can, so that we do not risk remaining separated from him forever.

Temptations

Different from sins are temptations to sin. We all have them. We feel an urge to eat too much, to drink too much alcohol, to lust after someone, to stay in bed when we should get up, to look at an internet site that we know is inappropriate, to use bad language…

How do temptations relate to our moral life? The very etymology of the word temptation gives us an answer. The word comes from the Latin word *tentatio*, which means simply a test, or a trial. So temptations are tests, tests of our resolve to do what we ought. As tests, temptations in themselves are not sinful. It is only when we give in to them that they become sinful.

Is it God who is tempting us? No, God does not tempt us, in the sense of putting us in a situation in which we are strongly inclined to offend him. He is too good a father to do that. St James writes: "Let no one say when he is tempted, 'I am tempted by God'; for God cannot be tempted with evil and he himself tempts no one; but each person is tempted when he is lured and enticed by his own desire" (*James* 1:13-14).

While God does not tempt us, he does allow us to be tempted. Why would he do that? Because temptations, as tests, reveal the strength of our virtue and love for God and they can be great sources of merit and sanctity. Let us not forget that Jesus himself underwent temptations in the desert before beginning his public life (cf. *Matthew* 4:1-11). After forty days of prayer and fasting, he was tempted by the devil in three different ways, but each time he rejected the temptation.

In so doing, he proved his love for the Father and gave us an example so that we too would be strong in resisting temptation. The Bible's *Letter to the Hebrews* says: "For we have not a high priest who is unable to sympathise with our weaknesses, but one who in every respect has been tempted as we are, yet without sinning. Let us then with confidence draw near to the throne of grace, that we may receive mercy and find grace to help in time of need" (*Hebrews* 4:15-16).

We know that God always gives us sufficient grace, or help, to overcome temptations. St Paul writes: "God is faithful, and he will not let you be tempted beyond your strength, but with the temptation will also provide the way of escape, that you may be able to endure it" (*1 Corinthians* 10:13). Perhaps St Paul was thinking of his own experience when, tempted by a "thorn" in the flesh, he begged God three times to be freed from it. He heard the consoling words, "My grace is sufficient for you, for my power is made perfect in weakness" (*2 Corinthians* 12:9). In every temptation, we can be assured that God will give us sufficient grace to overcome it.

Moreover, temptations can be very beneficial in the spiritual life. St Catherine of Siena, a fourteenth-century saint, records the following words from God as to why he allows us to be tempted: "The devil, dearest daughter, is the instrument of my justice to torment the souls who have miserably offended me. And I have set him in this life to tempt and molest my creatures, not for my creatures to be conquered, but that they may conquer, proving their virtue, and receive from me the glory of victory (*Dialogue*, 2.27). Indeed, God does not want us to be conquered, to fall into sin, but rather to conquer, to prove our virtue and receive from him the glory of victory, the crown of heaven.

St Augustine too writes: "Our pilgrim life here on earth cannot be without temptation, for it is through temptation that we make progress, and it is only by being tempted that we come to know ourselves. We cannot win our crown unless we overcome, and we cannot overcome unless we enter the contest and there is no contest unless we have an enemy and the temptations he brings" (*Discourses on the Psalms,* Ps 60, 2-3).

So, temptations are opportunities to show God how much we love him by struggling to overcome them. We should not look for temptations, but if they come, we have a great opportunity to grow in holiness, in love for God. In a word, temptations are both sources of sin and sources of sanctity.

4

The value of suffering

One of the great mysteries of life is suffering. Suffering is a reality. It is there in everyone's life. It takes a multitude of forms, from a sleepless night or a common cold to the chronic, severe pain of arthritis or cancer. These are forms of what we call *physical suffering*, suffering experienced primarily in the body. But then there is also the suffering that comes with the sickness or death of a loved one, the loss of a job, a broken relationship... These are what we call *moral* suffering, which is experienced not so much in the body as in the soul, in the heart. While one can make a theoretical distinction between physical and moral suffering, in practice they are often very interrelated. For example, sickness in the body can often result in anxiety, sadness or even depression in the soul. Conversely, sadness over a broken relationship can result in bodily sickness.

While most forms of suffering are simply part and parcel of everyday life, sometimes suffering is caused by the deliberate actions of others, even of those close to us: domestic violence, verbal abuse by someone we love, vandalism of our property, damage caused by a drunken driver... These are harder to take. But they too are part of life and we must find a way to deal with them. This often requires that we forgive the person who has made us suffer, hard though it may be. We will see more about this later in this book.

Naturally, we should do all we can to reduce or even eliminate suffering. Here the Catholic Church and the institutions of so many other religions have done marvellous work for centuries through their hospitals, aged care facilities, palliative care units, mental hospitals, assistance to those in prison, etc. But inevitably there will still be suffering in the lives of all of us. How we cope with it has a great bearing on how God will judge us in the final exam. There are those who complain about their suffering, curse it, and perhaps even get angry with God for allowing it. These people lose the merit they could have gained through suffering, and they even offend God by their attitude. Others accept suffering as part of God's plan for them, even embracing the cross of suffering, as Christ embraced the cross that brought him to death. These people gain much merit through it, and God will reward them for it in the judgment.

People with the same suffering can react very differently to it. One person rendered paraplegic by an accident may grieve over the loss of the use of his legs and spend the rest of his life feeling sorry for himself, while another may see the situation as a challenge for further growth and set out to achieve his goals within the limitations of his disability. I dare say we are all filled with admiration at the athletes competing in the Paralympics, who have risen above their suffering and have found a new meaning in life. I once saw an interview with a priest in his 30s who had been left quadriplegic after an automobile accident. In spite of having lost all movement from his neck down, after several years of rehabilitation he was able to return to his role of giving ethics classes in a university. Asked how he viewed his situation, he replied: "I feel like a millionaire who has lost a thousand dollars."

In this chapter I have set myself the task of attempting to draw meaning out of suffering from the Christian perspective. You may not be Christian, but I hope you will bear with me, since the Christian faith has much to offer everyone in seeing meaning in suffering, and I want to share it with you.

I must warn you from the outset that some of what I have to say may sound like blasphemy. Blasphemy, that is, not in the eyes of God, but in the eyes of our hedonistic society, which looks on pain and suffering as an unmitigated evil, to be avoided at all costs. Such a society looks on any attempt to find meaning in suffering as utter blasphemy. Indeed, when the pursuit of pleasure becomes the purpose of life, any effort to understand and accept suffering must be folly. But then, there is nothing new in this. St Paul, after all, wrote to the Corinthians 2000 years ago: "Here are the Jews asking for signs and wonders, here are the Greeks intent on their philosophy; but what we preach is Christ crucified; to the Jews, a discouragement, to the Gentiles, mere folly; but to us who have been called, Jew and Gentile alike, Christ the power of God, Christ the wisdom of God" (*1 Corinthians* 1:22-24).

The suffering of Jesus Christ

Where we catch a glimpse of the true meaning of suffering is in the suffering of Jesus Christ. In his conversation with a Jew named Nicodemus, Jesus says: "For God so loved the world that he gave his only Son, that whoever believes in him should not perish but have eternal life" (*John* 3:16). It was the love of God for man that moved him to send his Son Jesus to earth to die on a cross, in order to reconcile mankind with God. Through his death, Christ opened the way to eternal life, where there would be no more suffering.

Jesus really understood human suffering. He lived on earth as man for thirty-three years and, so to speak, entered the world of suffering. He experienced tiredness, hunger, thirst, misunderstanding, betrayal, the injustice of his condemnation, and especially the agony of his passion and death on the cross. He knew suffering in his own flesh.

He had compassion on those who suffered and helped many of them. He healed the sick, consoled the afflicted, fed the hungry, freed people from deafness, from blindness, from leprosy, from the devil and he even restored three people to life.

Yet it must be said that he did not come to free the world from suffering in its earthly dimension. Rather he came, as he said to Nicodemus, so that man should not perish but have eternal life. Man perishes, not when he suffers on earth in his body, but when he suffers eternally in hell and loses eternal life. Jesus accomplished this definitive liberation of mankind from suffering by undergoing intense, indescribable suffering on the cross. With his death, Jesus opened up for mankind the possibility of a life free from suffering in heaven.

The key to understanding the great mystery of Christ's suffering for the salvation of mankind, and indeed of man's suffering, is love. As we saw before, "So much did God love the world that he sent his only-begotten Son." Christ suffered out of love for mankind. St John, at the beginning of his account of Christ's suffering and death, says of Christ that, "having loved his own were in the world, he loved them to the end" (*John* 13:1). He also quotes Christ's words, "Greater love has no man than this, that a man lay down life for his friends" (*John* 15:13).

We see this in human suffering too. When a mother loves her children, she does not count the cost of getting up in the middle of the night to attend to their needs, to make a meal or do the laundry, even though she is exhausted.

Our own suffering too acquires new meaning when we bear it in union with the cross of Christ. In the words of Pope John Paul II, "Human suffering has reached its culmination in the Passion of Christ. And at the same time it has entered into a completely new dimension and a new order: it has been linked to love, to that love of which Christ spoke to Nicodemus, to that love which creates good, drawing it out by means of suffering, just as the supreme good of Redemption of the world was drawn from the Cross of Christ, and from that Cross constantly takes its beginning" (Apostolic Letter *Salvifici doloris*, 18).

Popular wisdom gives us the well-known adage, "Sacrifice is the touchstone of love." That is, love is seen to be genuine when it is manifested in sacrifice. God shows the depth of his love for man by the sacrifice of the cross. And man can show the depth of his love for God and for his fellow man by sacrifice and suffering borne with love.

We should always remember too that, whatever suffering we may have here on earth, it is nothing compared with the happiness that awaits us in heaven. St Paul writes in his letter to the Romans: "We are ... fellow heirs with Christ, provided we suffer with him in order that we may also be glorified with him. I consider that the sufferings of this present time are not worth comparing with the glory that is to be revealed in us" (*Romans* 8:17-18).

In view of all this, we can see that suffering, accepted with love, is not only not an unmitigated evil, but that much good can come from it. It can even be a blessing. Jesus tells us so when he pronounces those mysterious words in the Sermon on the Mount: "Blessed are those who mourn; they shall be comforted. ... Blessed are those who suffer persecution in the cause of right; the kingdom of heaven is theirs. Blessed are you, when men revile you, and persecute you, and speak all manner of evil against you falsely, because of me. Be glad and light-hearted, for a rich reward awaits you in heaven" *Matthew* 5:5, 10-12). Suffering, a blessing? If Christ says so, it must be so. In an effort to understand this, let us consider seven ways in which suffering can bring about much good, and even be a blessing. If we see it in this light and bear it well, we will be well prepared to face God in the judgment.

1. *Suffering strengthens character*

We all know people who have been through more than their "fair share" of suffering, and have emerged greatly strengthened in character by it: migrants who have left advantaged positions in their home country to flee persecution and who have had to start from scratch to rebuild their lives in a new country where they did not even know the language; business people who have lost everything and have had to start over from scratch, sometimes several times in the course of their career, finally ending up with very successful businesses; people who have overcome severe handicaps to lead lives of great happiness and usefulness to others... The world is full of such people, some well known and most known only to their family and friends, whose lives are a real inspiration to others. Their character, tempered in the forge of suffering, helped them go on to achieve great things. Without their suffering, they would not be the persons they came to be.

An eloquent personal testimony in this regard comes in a letter to a newspaper some years ago, written at a time when euthanasia was being proposed as a remedy for suffering:

> In 1959, as a three-year old I became a *grand mal* epileptic, having between 20-30 seizures per day. The diagnosis my parents received was that I would become more and more brain damaged and eventually die... Today, some would see such a heart-wrenching set of circumstances as justification for euthanasia...
>
> The epilepsy was eventually controlled with heavy doses of powerful medication. I did receive considerable brain damage and it took the best part of seven years before a semblance of normal functioning was reached... I have often seen my life as worthless and wished to die. Yet, on mature reflection, as I approach 40, I am glad that euthanasia did not exist. There is a certain dignity in struggling against obstacles and slowly but certainly overcoming them.
>
> My objection to euthanasia is precisely because it takes away the pain and struggle. It is a quick fix. I have a soul and that soul is not strengthened by instant gratification and the avoidance of pain. It is made worthy by suffering borne well and by living a difficult life with some dignity. My objection to euthanasia is that it substitutes dignity of circumstances for dignity of character. Dignity of character shines out of pain well endured – not out of

pain sanitised, avoided and dismissed" (*The Australian,* 2 June 1995).

2. Suffering helps one to be more sympathetic towards others who are suffering.

People react to the suffering of others in different ways. Some turn their heads and quickly leave the scene, incapable of relating to the person who is suffering, while others immediately enter into a close relationship. There can be no question but that a person who has been through suffering himself or herself finds it much easier to relate to the suffering of others.

In western society in general, we are not used to suffering on the scale experienced in many parts of the less affluent world, where hunger, poor standards of health, natural disasters, war, etc., have made people used to considerable levels of suffering. In those countries, when people are suffering, their family members and friends do not flee but rather embrace them, sit with them and give them comfort. In our own society, where in general there is comparatively little suffering, we are not used to suffering and we find it difficult to relate to the suffering of others.

An acquaintance of mine in Melbourne, whose husband died of a brain tumour some years ago after four months in a hospice, told me that no fewer than three of her friends had asked her if she was going to have her husband "put away". "Hasn't he suffered enough already?" they asked. The truth of the matter is that the man was not suffering at all. Nor was his wife, who was happy to be able to visit him every day. The three friends, she said, were all young, in their 30s, and all wealthy. "They are just selfish", she said. Perhaps she was right. They don't know what it means to suffer and they flee from it, hiding their own fear of suffering under the cloak of a seemingly altruistic desire to prevent someone else's suffering.

When we have suffered ourselves, we find it much easier to feel true compassion for others who are suffering. The word "compassion", after all, comes from Latin words meaning "to suffer with". We can then more easily "suffer with the suffering", in the words of a first-century Christian document, the *Didache*. This compassion will give those who are suffering more strength and support than the detached "pity" which only knows how to look on suffering from a distance, much as one looks on a suffering animal with pity. What people who are suffering need is compassion, accompaniment, love, not mere pity, and those who have suffered themselves are better able to show it to them.

3. Suffering brings people closer to God

One of the most natural responses of people who are suffering, or who are close to the suffering of others, is to pray. Even people who have hardly prayed before turn to God in these moments. We see it, for example, in war time. As they say, there are no atheists in foxholes. Faced with the prospect of imminent death, be it in war, an earthquake, a flood, a wild fire, or the diagnosis of an aggressive cancer, knowing that there is little that can be done humanly, people turn naturally to God. We saw this in *Dying to Live* in some of the near-death experiences, when people with no religion at all thought they were dying and began to pray. Without this danger or suffering, they would often have remained distant from God.

Those who have read *Dying to Live* may have noticed that I dedicated the book to Ellie, a girl who was diagnosed with an aggressive brain tumour at the age of fifteen and who died at the age of twenty, very much looking forward to meeting God. Her sickness brought not only Ellie, but her whole family, much closer to God. For them, Ellie's sickness was distressing from a human point of view, but a real blessing in the spiritual sense. What is more, thousands of copies of a card with a photograph of this beautiful girl and a prayer for her were printed and distributed widely. One was handed personally to Pope Francis and a Spanish translation of the prayer was distributed in Mexico and Spain. In Ellie's school, the 600 girls from infants to secondary said the prayer for her in their classrooms each morning for five years. The thousands of people who prayed for Ellie were drawn closer to God by their prayer. Who said suffering wasn't a blessing?

Christians, and others who value Christ's life and teachings, can also find that suffering unites them closely with Jesus Christ himself. We have already seen how Jesus, by taking human nature and living on earth for thirty-three years, and especially by his own suffering and death, entered the world of suffering. He is especially close to those who suffer. To everyone, no matter what their religious belief. Indeed, Jesus invited those who wanted to follow him to take up the cross of their own suffering: "If anyone would come after me, let him deny himself and take up his cross and follow me" (*Matthew* 16:24). And he assures us that if we do this, the cross will not be heavy: "Come to me, all who labour and are heavy laden, and I will give you rest. Take my yoke upon you, and learn from me; for I am gentle and lowly in heart and you shall find rest for your souls. For my yoke is easy, and my burden is light" (*Matthew* 11:28-30).

St Paul gives us the testimony of his own identification with Christ through the cross: "I have been crucified with Christ; it is no longer I who live, but Christ who lives in me" (*Galatians* 2:20). By taking up his cross, that is, by willingly accepting suffering of whatever kind, the sufferer has the consolation of knowing that he is especially close to Jesus Christ. A person who understood this well was a Canberra mother of six children who was dying of cancer in 1987. One day she wrote in her diary, addressing herself to Christ:

> The pain in my chest is crushing me. As the pain crushed You as You struggled to breathe while you hung on the Cross. You are in my pain. I am in Yours. We are one – my God and I! What else can I ever ask for? In this You have given me proof of your love."

This woman was greatly consoled by seeing herself united with Christ in the midst of her great pain. Without that awareness, her pain might have seemed meaningless, and even cruel.

4. *Suffering is a manifestation of God's love*

The Canberra woman's example of loving acceptance of suffering has already suggested a further way in which suffering is a blessing: it is a manifestation of God's love. Perhaps the statement can appear somewhat startling. Suffering, a manifestation of God's love? Would God allow those he loves to suffer? He himself says so. In the book of *Revelation* in the Bible God says, "Those whom I love, I reprove and chasten; so be zealous and repent" (*Revelation* 3:19). And in the *Letter to the Hebrews*: "For the Lord disciplines him whom he loves, and chastises every son whom he receives… God is treating you as sons; for what son is there whom his father does not discipline?" (*Hebrews* 12:6-7) Just as earthly fathers discipline their children, making them suffer in some way in order to correct them and teach them virtue, so God treats his children on earth in the same way. Moreover, as the Letter goes on to say, our earthly fathers "disciplined us for a short time at their pleasure, but he disciplines us for our good, that we may share his holiness" (*Hebrews* 12:10). Whatever allows us to share in God's holiness must surely be a blessing, even if it is painful at the time.

What God is saying here applies in the first place to his own beloved Son, Jesus Christ. Christ suffered more than we ever will and he was the most beloved of his Father God. Many of the saints down the ages were told by God that they would have much to suffer on his account. Indeed, St John Vianney, the nineteenth-century French priest known more commonly as the Curé of Ars, says that the greatest saints were those who suffered the most. He himself would have to be numbered among them. In another place he says: "You wonder why God, who is goodness itself, allows us to suffer. .

. But what would you think of a doctor who lost his patient because he was afraid to give him the necessary but unpleasant treatment?"

We may find it difficult to understand why God allows us to suffer, but we can only trust that he is doing it for a good reason. Perhaps only at the end of our life will we understand it. The little poem "The Weaver" explains it well:

> My life is but a weaving
> Between my Lord and me.
> I cannot choose the colours;
> He worketh steadily.
>
> Oftimes He weaveth sorrow,
> And I in foolish pride
> Forget He sees the upper,
> And I the underside.
>
> Not 'til the loom is silent
> and the shuttles cease to fly,
> Shall God unroll the canvas
> and explain the reason why.
>
> The dark threads are as needful
> In the Weaver's skilful hand,
> As the threads of gold and silver
> In the pattern He has planned.

5. Suffering can help to make up for our sins

As we saw in the chapter on purgatory in *Dying to Live,* we need to do so something in this life to make up for our sins, or we will do it in purgatory. Naturally, we could never make up fully for even the slightest offence against almighty God, nor does he require it, but he does ask us to do something. This is the reason for the penance, or self-denial, which has been part of the life of Christians from the beginning. Christians live Lent as a season of self-denial, including fasting, before Easter, accompanying Christ on the cross in preparation for his resurrection.

The need of making up for wrongdoing is understood by everyone. It is a matter of natural justice, and it forms part of the legal system of every human society. Those who have been found guilty of crimes are sentenced to time in prison or to some form of community service. It is thus not surprising that it should also form part of man's relationship with God. By the infinite mercy of God and the death of Jesus Christ on the cross, the penance we must do is much less than our sins deserve, but nonetheless we must still do some form of penance.

We can do this by such ancient – and modern – practices as fasting and by other forms of self-denial in food and drink, entertainment, comfort, etc. We can also do it by offering to God whatever suffering we may have in life, big or small. Christ invited us to follow him along the path of self-denial: "If any man would come after me, let him deny himself and take up his cross daily and follow me" (*Luke* 9:23). The cross we take up may be both those we voluntarily choose, and also those sufferings which life brings. If, instead of complaining about our suffering, we accept it willingly and offer it to God, it helps greatly to make up for our sins. And to shorten our time in purgatory, if indeed we needed to go there. In this sense too suffering can be a great blessing.

6. *Suffering can be offered up for others*

Every person of faith understands the value of praying for others. Perhaps fewer understand that they can also offer their work, their relaxation, and especially their suffering as a most powerful prayer for others. When a person is suffering very much, the awareness that the suffering is benefitting someone else can be very consoling.

I was told some time ago about a retired university professor living out his last years in a Sydney nursing home, who felt very sorry for himself and saw no purpose in his continuing existence. But then he was visited by some boys from a nearby boys' club who asked him if he would offer his suffering for their work in leading their friends closer to God. The professor brightened up and thereafter looked forward to the boys' visits, asking them how their work was going. He was happy to know that somehow his sufferings were helping others. His life, which had become purposeless, had taken on a new meaning.

7. Suffering benefits the carers

One of the things we see when there is a natural disaster, not only in our own city or country, but even in other parts of the world, is the outpouring of generosity by those not directly affected. People donate money, time, clothing, food, blankets, whatever is needed, to alleviate the suffering of others. This benefits greatly those who give.

On a more personal level, anyone who has spent time caring for someone who was sick, elderly or dying will agree that they have grown humanly in many ways through their work. Really, practically everyone is called upon to look after a suffering person from time to time, be it only to attend to a sick person at home. One virtue which can be greatly tested and thereby grow through such work is that of patience. Compassion is another quality that carers generally have to a great degree and which grows through their work. And what can one not say about generosity, resourcefulness, cheerfulness, kindness...?

Health workers benefit not only by looking after the sick and suffering, but also by improving their professional skills, as they are forced to confront ever new situations and medical conditions. Through their dedication, the suffering are much better looked after today than they were years ago. It is frightening to think what the state of health care would be today if suffering people were simply assisted to end their life, or were left to die rather than having efforts made to improve their care.

Carers can also grow spiritually through their work. They can consider that what they are doing for others is done to Jesus Christ himself. He said so: "I was hungry and you gave me food, I was thirsty and you gave me drink... I was sick and you visited me... Truly, I say to you, as you did it to one of the least of my brethren, you did it to me" (*Matthew* 25:35-36, 40). This care for another, as done to Jesus, makes the person more deserving of eternal life. Again, Jesus said so: "Come, O blessed of my Father, inherit the kingdom prepared for you from the foundation of the world; for I was hungry and you gave me drink..." (*Matthew* 25:34-35). It is truly a blessing to be dealing with Jesus himself and meriting heaven through one's care for the suffering. Mother Teresa of Calcutta was a great believer in this reality. She tells this story:

> One day they brought a man from the streets and half of his body was all eaten up; worms were crawling all over his body, and nobody could stand near him, the odour was so great. So I went to clean him and he looked at me, and then he asked: "Why do you do this? Everybody has given me away. Why do you do this? Why do you come near me?" "I love you", I said. "I love you. You are Jesus in a distressing disguise. Jesus is sharing his passion with you." And he looked up at me and said, "And you – you too, by doing what you are doing, are sharing." I said, "No, I am sharing the joy of loving with you. I love the Jesus in you." And this Hindu gentleman, so full of suffering, what did he say? "Glory be to Jesus Christ." There was no complaint of those big worms eating into his body. There was no crying, no calling. He realised that he was somebody, that he was loved (Address to priests, Rome, 5-9 October 1984).

In view of all this, it is clear that suffering, far from being an unmitigated evil, can have many benefits, both for the sufferers and for their carers. If we understand the meaning of suffering in this way, we can come to welcome it, even to love it. One person who saw it in this light was the founder of the Catholic prelature Opus Dei, St Josemaría Escrivá, who himself had much suffering in his life. When he was only thirty, he wrote in a notebook:

> Jesus, I feel such desires for making reparation. My role is to love and suffer. But love makes me rejoice in suffering, to such an extent that it now seems impossible for me ever to suffer. I told you before that no one could make me upset. And I would even add that no one can make me suffer, because suffering brings me joy and peace (*Intimate Notes,* 24 January 1932).

If we receive suffering well, it can be a big part of our credentials when we face God in the judgment. It can help us pass the final exam. Let us not waste it.

5

The worship of God

The Ten Commandments

What we have seen in the previous chapters is the foundations of our moral life, the aspects that have a bearing on our moral life in general. In this chapter and the following ones we will study in detail particular moral precepts. We will follow roughly the order of these precepts as given by God to Moses in the Ten Commandments, around the thirteenth century BC. While they form part of the Judaeo-Christian heritage, the commandments are common to peoples and religions all over the world. Everywhere people are taught to honour their parents, not to kill the innocent, not to steal or tell lies, and so on.

The moral teachings of the commandments are based on the natural law, and hence they are common to all peoples. God gave them to us to show us the way to happiness and to heaven. He is a loving father and so he revealed his law to us to make it easier to follow the pathway that leads to heaven. The second-century Christian writer St Irenaeus points out how the Ten Commandments are related to the natural law: "From the beginning, God had implanted in the heart of man the precepts of the natural law. Then he was content to remind him of them. This was the Decalogue" (*Adv. haeres.* 4, 15, 1). The word "Decalogue", by the way, comes from the Greek, meaning literally "ten words". It is another name for the Ten Commandments.

As they are based on the natural law, the commandments oblige everyone, since everyone has human nature. They involve norms of conduct regarding respect for life, treating others fairly, not killing the innocent, not stealing others' property, and so on. They express our fundamental duties towards God and our fellow human beings and, as such, provide a sure guide for our conduct on the way to heaven.

It is interesting to note that Jesus himself spoke about the importance of keeping the commandments if someone wants to be found worthy of heaven. To a young man who asked him, "Teacher, what good deed must I do, to have eternal life?" Jesus answered: "If you would enter life, keep the commandments" (*Matthew* 19:16-19). So, a great deal is at stake if we want to enjoy eternal life with God in heaven. And, to be sure, if we want to enjoy life here on earth too.

Having seen in *Dying to Live* that Jesus Christ claimed to be God and showed by his miracles, especially his resurrection from the dead, that he was God, we can regard him at least as a religious leader worthy of credence, so we will make frequent use of his teaching and his example. In that way we can strive to live our lives accordingly and be very well prepared when we face God in the judgment.

The first commandment

The first precept of the Ten Commandments refers to the worship of God. That is to be expected, since it was God who brought us into existence, who loves us and watches over us with his divine providence, and who has a place for all of us in heaven. He is, as we sometimes hear, our beginning and our end. Our first duty is to him.

The commandment to love and worship God is readily understood since, as we have seen, all peoples have a natural tendency to believe in some form of God. Although there are, admittedly, a good number of atheists and others who say they don't have any religion, the reality is that every civilisation has had some form of belief in God, some religion.

Some may have believed in a multiplicity of gods, or in a god identified with nature, or in a god who didn't care about man, but all have had some form of religion, some belief in a being beyond themselves. Many of these religions had a priesthood, prayers, sacrifices, rituals, etc. In short, man is by nature a religious being. He has a natural desire for God, written in his heart. If we took a poll and asked people whether they were looking for God, many would answer flatly no. But deep down, everyone is looking for God. How can we say this? We see it in the natural tendencies of the intellect and will, which all human beings have.

The intellect, or mind, has a natural desire for truth and it does not stop searching until it finds the answer to the most fundamental questions. Questions like: What is the origin of the universe, with all its harmony and complexity? What is the meaning of life? Is there life after death? Is there a God, who somehow controls the world and who is responsible for my destiny? The answer to these deeper questions is ultimately God himself.

The will, sometimes referred to as the heart, – the faculty by which we choose, desire, love, etc., – has a natural desire for the good, and with it for happiness. It finds happiness when it finds a good. But finite, limited goods like money, possessions, fame, etc., cannot fully satisfy the longings of the heart. We see this in the many wealthy, influential, people who are not happy at all. The will is spiritual, in some way unlimited, and ultimately only the infinite good, God himself, can fully satisfy it.

For this reason, St Augustine (354-430 AD) wrote, speaking to God: "For you have made us for yourself, and our heart is restless until it rests in you" (*Confessions* 1, 1, 1). A little later in that same work, his *Confessions*, he says: "When I am completely united to you, there will be no more sorrow or trials; entirely full of you, my life will be complete" (*Confessions* 10, 28, 39).

Indeed, everyone wants to be happy. But only God can fully

satisfy the longing for happiness. Therefore, everyone, whether they know it or not, is looking for God. This has led people of all civilisations to search for meaning, for an understanding of the world around them, for the origin and meaning of their existence. It has led them to believe in some form of supreme being who can satisfy their deepest desires and to worship him.

So belief in God as the origin and end of our being is common throughout history, and the worship of God is therefore the first of our moral obligations. Indeed, the first three of the ten commandments relate to the worship of God, specifying different aspects of that worship, and the last seven relate to love for our neighbour. Jesus himself summarised them when he was asked which commandment was the greatest. He answered: "You shall love the Lord your God with all your heart, and with all your soul, and with all your mind. This is the greatest and first commandment. And a second is like it: You shall love your neighbour as yourself. On these two commandments hang all the Law and the prophets" (*Matthew* 22:37-40).

This same teaching comes in the Old Testament of the Bible. Moses, having received the commandments from God, told the people: "Now this is the commandment, the statutes and the ordinances which the Lord your God commanded me to teach you ... Hear, O Israel: The Lord our God is one Lord; and you shall love the Lord your God with all your heart, and with all your soul, and with all your might" (*Deuteronomy* 6:1, 4-5).

The actual text of the first commandment is: "I am the Lord your God: you shall not have strange gods before me" (*Exodus* 20:2-3). The commandment, in simple terms, commands us to worship the one true God and to avoid sins against this worship, especially by worshiping false gods. How can we fulfil this commandment?

One day you are going to meet God in the judgment, so one of the first things you can do is get to know him beforehand. Depending on your present state of religious belief, you can go back and read the religious books on which you were brought up. In any case, since there is only one God and this God has made himself known in the Bible, you can obtain a copy of that book. The first part of the Bible, as we saw in *Dying to Live,* is the Old Testament, which begins with a description of how the world came to be. The Old Testament is common to both Jews and Christians. It relates the history of the Jewish people throughout the centuries, and contains many beautiful ideas on the good life, especially in such books as the Psalms, Proverbs and Wisdom.

The New Testament contains books about the life of Christ in the Gospels, a history of the early Church in the Acts of the Apostles, and numerous writings by St Paul and others on the principal teachings of Christ. Although you may not be Christian, these books are still of great value, since they contain much teaching on the good life and, in the end, they come from God himself. What is more, Christianity is numerically the largest religion in the world, so its teachings deserve to be known.

Apart from getting to know God, you can and should follow the natural inclination to worship him, as people of all religions have done. If you believe in a supreme being who has created the universe, who has your destiny in his hands, and who will judge you at the end of your life, it is only natural to have a personal relationship with him, and to worship him. You can do this in many ways.

A first and fundamental way is prayer. Prayer is simply talking with God. It can take the various forms of simply conversing with him in your own words, saying prayers you have learned in the past which are common in your religion, telling God you love him, asking him for favours, thanking him for the many blessings he has given you, and telling him you are sorry for having offended him.

Also very important is to beg God to forgive your sins, your offences against both him and others. We have all done many things in life which we knew were wrong and, if we want to go to heaven with God, we must be sorry for those offences. As we saw in *Dying to Live,* if we want to avoid hell, we must be truly sorry for our sins. This sorrow must be genuine, with a true conversion of heart. Implied in this sorrow is the resolution to try not to commit the offence again, even though we know that, in our human weakness, we may very well commit it again. What is important is the resolution to be determined to avoid doing it in the future. Repentance must be a real conversion of heart, a rejection of sin, not just a passing thought or sentiment.

When God sees our sorrow, our repentance and desire to change, his merciful love will move him to forgive us. And we shouldn't wait until the end of our life to ask for this forgiveness. We don't know how long we have to live, even though we may be young and healthy. Now is the time for sorrow, so that we can be well prepared to meet God when he calls us into the next life.

We can also worship God by exercising the virtue of faith, or belief in God and all that he has taught. We do this by seeking to know what he has taught and believing it, knowing that God is truth and that he can neither deceive, nor be deceived. We should not admit any doubts about such basic truths as whether God exists, whether he is telling us the truth, whether there is life after death, etc. And, of course, we should not deny that God exists, through any form of atheism. We saw scientific evidence for the existence of God, based on various aspects of the universe, in chapter 5 of *Dying to Live,* so it is not difficult to believe in him.

We also worship God through the virtue of hope, trusting that God will give us all the help we need to be faithful to his law in order to be taken heaven when we die. Here we must avoid sins against hope, the two most important of which are despair, where we do not trust that God will forgive our sins and give us the help we need; and presumption, where we presume that we can save ourselves without his help, or that he will save us without any effort on our part.

We worship God too through the virtue of love, or charity, which inclines us to love God with our whole heart. Since God is love and the source of all love, and since he loves every single one of us and wants us to be saved, it is easy to love him. We must avoid offending God by any hatred of him, lack of gratitude for his many gifts, or by negligence in our spiritual life, sometimes called lukewarmness.

We must struggle too to avoid offending God by worshiping false gods. This would include, of course, worshiping Satan through involvement in satanic activities, but also putting some other good ahead of our worship of God, by giving undue importance to earning money and acquiring possessions, excelling at sport, pursuing pleasure, etc. To do so would be in effect to worship the false god of wealth, sport, success in human endeavours, etc.

Other ways of offending God in this area include using extraordinary means to know what we cannot know by natural means. For example, by attending séances, consulting horoscopes, palm readers, clairvoyants, using Ouija boards and tarot cards, etc. We should avoid unhealthy curiosity in this area, and simply put our trust in God, knowing that he will show us whatever we need to know.

Another sin against the first commandment is what is known as tempting God. It consists in putting God's goodness and almighty power to the test by word or deed. In a word, it is to hope for an unusual manifestation of God's power, for example by expecting God to help us pass an exam when we haven't studied, or to help us reach our destination safely when we are driving recklessly.

The second commandment

The second commandment is, "You shall not take the name of the Lord your God in vain." It commands us to use the name of God with respect, and never to treat it with scorn. This is understandable. Once we know who God is, how he created the universe out of nothing, and how he loves us and forgives us, we are naturally inclined to speak of him and use his name with the greatest respect. Even though the first commandment, which refers to giving due worship to God, implicitly includes honouring the divine name, God wanted to emphasise the importance of his name by giving us a separate commandment relating to it. We read in one of the psalms of the Old Testament: "O Lord, our Lord, how majestic is your name in all the earth!" (*Psalms* 8:1)

In human affairs we reveal our name to others only when we have a certain relationship of trust with them. God, upon entering into a close relationship with his people in Old Testament times, revealed his name to Moses, calling himself Yahweh, which can be translated as, "I am who I am" (*Exodus* 3:14). What we learn from this is that God is not an anonymous force; he is a person, he has a name. And he wants us to know, trust and love him. He is making himself accessible to us, so that we can know him more intimately and address him personally. This applies to all of us, to every single human being. God loves everyone. He has a place in heaven for all of us and he wants us to be with him there.

So the second commandment commands us to use God's name with respect and to witness to it by professing our faith before others without fear. It forbids misusing that name by blasphemy, which consists in uttering against God, inwardly or outwardly, any words that would imply hatred, disrespect or defiance, or in speaking ill of God. At the same time, it is good to know that to say, "O my God!", for example when witnessing an accident, is not blasphemy, but rather an expression of piety, of respect for God. It is as if we were saying, "O my God, help this person".

One way in which we may legitimately use the name of God is in taking an oath. For example, some take the oath of office when they assume a role in the service of the public. Here they call upon the name of God as they swear to carry out the duties of their office to the best of their ability, "so help me God." Others may take an oath when they appear in court, swearing "to tell the truth, the whole truth and nothing but the truth, so help me God". Naturally, there is nothing wrong with this, but the person must never take a false oath by lying, not intending to carry out what they are swearing to do. If someone lies under oath in court it is the very serious sin, and usually a crime as well, of perjury.

Apart from these situations, in general we should avoid taking unnecessary oaths. For example, we should not ask someone to swear he is telling the truth when we do not trust him. Jesus referred to this when he said, "You have heard that it was said to the men of old, 'You shall not swear falsely, but shall perform to the Lord what you have sworn.' But I say to you, do not swear at all... Let what you say be simply 'Yes' or 'No'; anything more than this comes from the evil one" (*Mattthew* 5:33-34).

The third commandment

The third commandment, also related to the worship of God, is "Remember to keep holy the Lord's Day." Many religions have a particular day of the week on which their adherents worship God by attending a religious service. For Christians it is Sunday, the day of Christ's resurrection from the dead. For Jews it is Saturday, the seventh day of the week, on which God "rested" after his six days of "work" in creating the world. And for Muslims it is Friday, the day on which they believe Adam was created, he entered the garden of paradise and was expelled from it, and it is the day of the last hour, or resurrection.

In any case, we should find some way to worship God, to show him that we love him, to ask him for favours, thank him for his many gifts and tell him we are sorry for having offended him. If your religion has a form of communal worship in a particular place and on a particular day, by all means try to attend it. It is there that you worship God in accordance with your beliefs in the company of others, usually led by a minister of your religion. Nothing is so natural as to worship the God who loves you and who wants you to be with him in heaven. And the fact that you worship along with others is a big help to everyone. It shows that you are not alone on your faith journey, and those others will support you on your way.

If you do not have a communal form of worship, you can always worship God on your own, however you see fit. Or you can seek out some other community of faith and ask if you can join them.

Returning to the Bible, God told the ancient Jews that the seventh day of the week was a sabbath of solemn rest, holy to the Lord (cf. *Exodus* 31:15). By the way, the word sabbath, from which we derive the words Saturday and sabbatical, means precisely *rest*.

The first Christians began to worship God on the first day of the week, Sunday. They did this for several reasons. As we have seen, it was on Sunday that Jesus rose from the dead. But Sunday was also the first day of creation, and being also the eighth day, it symbolises the new creation ushered in by Christ's Resurrection. St Justin, a philosopher who died a martyr in the middle of the second century, explains this practice: "We all gather on the day of the sun, for it is the first day [after the Jewish sabbath, but also the first day] when God, separating matter from darkness, made the world; and on this same day Jesus Christ our Saviour rose from the dead" (*1 Apol.* 67).

Christians who may not be inclined to attend a religious service on Sunday can consider how good God has been to them in becoming man and dying on the cross for them, and how much he has blessed them throughout the week. The least they can do on Sunday is make the sacrifice to attend a service to worship him, thank him for all his blessings, and ask him to help them in many ways. In this context they can remember Christ's question to the apostles in the Garden of Gethsemane, "Could you not watch with me one hour"? (*Matthew* 26:40) Surely, we can find one hour a week to worship the God who has watched over us with his loving providence twenty-four hours, seven days a week.

Obviously, there can be reasons why someone may not be able to attend a service on a given day, and then they can consider themselves excused. Such reasons may be the fact that they are sick, that they have to look after a sick family member, that there is no service in their area, that they have to work on that day, etc.

For Jews and Christians as a matter of obligation, and for others too, it is also good to abstain from unnecessary work on the day of the religious service. In that way, they can spend more time with their family, visit relatives and friends, have more time to pray, relax and obtain much-needed rest, get some exercise, and so on. Naturally, family needs – for example the need to prepare meals – or other important services can excuse someone from this highly desirable rest.

This concludes our study of the first three commandments, all of which refer to the worship of God. After God, our next love is for our neighbour, considered in the broad sense as all of our fellow human beings. That is our next topic.

6

Love for our neighbour

After love for God and the obligation to worship him comes love for others here on earth, our neighbours. We recall Christ's words about the two greatest commandments: "You shall love the Lord your God with all your heart, and with all your soul, and with all your mind. This is the greatest and first commandment. And a second is like it: You shall love your neighbour as yourself. On these two commandments hang all the Law and the prophets" (*Matthew* 22:37-40).

The last seven commandments refer to specific obligations as regards love for others, and we will consider them in the chapters that follow. Here we will consider some general aspects of love for others, ones not contained specifically in any of the commandments.

But first, we can recall what we read in *Dying to Live* about people who have had a near-death experience. One of the most common reactions they had was the realisation that they should love more. They experienced the overwhelming love of God in heaven, along with an indescribable joy, and they were moved to want to love others more here on earth. We all tend to be somewhat selfish, concerned first and foremost with our own needs and interests. But when someone has experienced the life beyond, and especially God's love in heaven, they come back transformed, aware that they should now share God's love with others.

For the rest of us, who have not had a near-death experience, we might find it somewhat harder to know the importance of loving others, but we should strive to live it nonetheless. And rather than needing a commandment to love others, which of course exists, we should truly want to love them. Most people do. Children usually grow up in a loving family, where they experience the love of their parents and siblings, and they don't need to be told to love their family members in return. They naturally do so. They respond to the love that is shown them by loving those who have loved them. This love extends gradually to all the others who love them: relatives, friends, teachers, teammates, etc.

This alerts us to the principle that those who have the first claim on our love are those closest to us. This begins in the immediate family and gradually extends to others in our circle of relationships. Any right-minded person realises that this is the case. We readily understand that it would be wrong, for example, to spend many hours a week attending to strangers if that meant we neglected our spouse and children. They have the first claim on our love.

Love for strangers and "enemies"

But we should also show love for strangers and, in many people, there is a natural inclination to do so. If we see someone fall in the street, we are naturally inclined to help them. If we witness an accident, we see what we can do to help anyone who may be injured. If we see someone sick or homeless, we are moved to help them in any way we can.

One of the most inspiring examples of this in recent times was Mother Teresa of Calcutta, the Catholic nun who dedicated her life to helping the sick and homeless through the Missionaries of Charity she founded in 1950. She began her work in Calcutta but it is now spread throughout the world. She often referred to the people she helped as "the poorest of the poor".

We have already seen one account of her work in the chapter on suffering. In that same address to priests in 1984, she told how the President of Yemen had invited the Missionaries of Charity to work with the lepers in that Muslim country. She relates:

> There are many, many lepers. So we went to see the place and I saw there an open grave. The smell, the rottenness of the bodies, I cannot express what I saw. And I was thinking, Jesus how can you live here like that? And then I accepted that place. And if you went now you would see quite a different place. There's not a single Catholic there, and I asked one of the rich men, "These are all Muslim people. They need to pray. Kindly build a mosque for them, so they can pray". And the man was surprised that I, a Catholic sister, would ask such a thing, but they built a most beautiful mosque for the people. And you can see the lepers crawling, crawling, crawling, going there and praying. When the mosque was completely opened, he turned to me and said, "I give you my word, the next thing I will build here is a Catholic church for the sisters."

Admittedly, not everyone is capable of loving like Mother Teresa, nor are we obliged to do so, but it is helpful to see how far this love can go in a truly remarkable, generous person.

Another example of helping total strangers involved a family with five children, friends of mine, who were going on a trip around Australia, towing a campervan behind their car. When they had gone a day's journey and were hundreds of kilometres from Sydney, the suspension on the campervan broke and they could no longer tow it. While they looked at it in dismay, the cars whizzed past on the highway. Then one car, which had driven past, stopped and came back to them. The driver, a woman, asked if they needed help. When they explained their plight, she invited the whole family to her nearby farm and put them up for the night, giving them dinner and beds. The following day, while the husband drove back to Sydney to collect a new van, his children enjoyed themselves playing with the woman's children and experiencing life on a farm. The family stayed a second night and were finally on their way again, with immense gratitude to the woman and her family. She was a modern-day "good Samaritan", as in the parable told by Jesus (cf. *Luke* 10:25-37).

Jesus Christ went one step farther and invited us to love even our enemies. In his Sermon on the Mount he said:

> You have heard that it was said, "You shall love your neighbour and hate your enemy." But I say to you, Love your enemies and pray for those who persecute you, so that you may be sons of your Father who is in heaven; for he makes his sun rise on the evil and on the good, and sends rain on the just and on the unjust. For if you love those who love you, what reward have you? Do not even the tax collectors do the same? And if you salute only your brethren, what more are you doing than others? Do not even the Gentiles do the same? You, therefore, must be perfect, as your heavenly Father is perfect (*Matthew* 5:43-48).

Loving your enemies would have to be one of the most demanding precepts ever given. We all find it easy to love those who love us, and we can even love strangers, but no one finds it easy to love someone who has hurt us, someone we might consider an enemy.

One of the many people who have done this is Saint Josemaría Escrivá (1902-1975), the founder of Opus Dei. In the years just after the Spanish Civil War (1936-1939) he found himself in a taxi discussing with the driver the events that had led up to the war, which saw the killing of a million people, including 6000 priests. He said that it was a shame that the divisions had led to a war, and that it would have been better for the opposing sides to discuss their differences and live in peace with each other. The taxi driver had a very different view, and asked Saint Josemaría if he had been in Madrid during the war. When he answered yes, the driver said, "What a shame they didn't kill you!" Escrivá's response was to ask the driver if he had any children. When he answered yes, Saint Josemaría took out some extra money in addition to the fare and gave it to him to buy lollies for his children.

A final point to help us understand what loving our enemies means is that Jesus did not say we should *like* our enemies, for their ill treatment of us makes us naturally dislike them. He said we should *love* them, which consists in praying for them, wishing them well, not evil, and yes, forgiving them.

Forgiving others

Forgiving them? When they have hurt us so much? Yes, forgiving them. Again, we should understand what we mean by this. In simple terms, we could say that to forgive someone is to tell God, and ideally them too, that we don't hold anything against them, that we wish them well, not harm, that we love them, that we pray for them. Forgiveness is an act of the will, relieving the other person of any debt against us. It is not a feeling of kindness towards the person. When we think of what they have done, we will probably feel angry for quite some time. This is not a sign that we have not forgiven, but simply a natural response of our feelings.

We can learn much about forgiveness from the teaching of Jesus Christ. In the Sermon on the Mount he taught us to pray the well-known prayer, the *Our Father* (*Matthew* 6:9-13). In it we say, "Forgive us our trespasses as we forgive those who trespass against us." In other words, Jesus is saying that if we want God the Father to forgive our sins, our trespasses, we must first forgive those who have hurt us.

The great importance of forgiving is made clear when Jesus goes on to say, "For if you forgive men their trespasses, your heavenly Father also will forgive you; but if you do not forgive men their trespasses, neither will your Father forgive your trespasses" (*Matthew* 6:14-15). These are strong words and a reminder that forgiveness of others is essential if we expect God to forgive us. They are strong but they make sense. If we have not forgiven someone, we have closed our heart to them, our heart has become hardened, and it is closed also to the forgiveness God wants to give us. So, let us strive to forgive everyone who has hurt us throughout our life. After all, one day we are going to face God in the judgment, the final exam, and we desperately want God to forgive us so we can go to heaven.

But what if someone has hurt us not just once, but many times? Isn't there a limit to how often we must forgive them? The answer is clear. We must be ready to forgive them not once or twice, but always. There is an interesting passage in the Bible in which St Peter asked Jesus how often he should forgive his brother, if as many as seven times. Jesus answered: "I do not say to you seven times, but seventy times seven" (*Mt* 18:22). By the way, the number seven in Scripture refers to plenitude, fullness, and here it means an indefinite number. So we must be ready to forgive our neighbour always, no matter how many times he offends us. This is not easy, but it is essential.

It is very important to forgive those who have hurt us. If we haven't forgiven, we carry a grudge, hard feelings in our heart and this is not pleasant. Whenever we think of what someone has done to us, we only revive the anger. For this reason, it is helpful to reject quickly any thoughts of the offence the person has committed against us, since these thoughts can reopen the wound and prolong the hard feelings. The sooner we get over reminding ourselves of the offence, the better. They say "forgive and forget". But while we can always forgive, it is not easy to forget, nor is forgetting necessary for our forgiveness to be genuine. At the same time, it is also true that the less we think about the offence, the more quickly we will forget it.

What we don't want to do is go to our grave with the burden of not having forgiven someone. We want to free ourselves of that burden before we die. It is a source of great joy and peace to do so. There is a beautiful line in the Roland Joffé film "There be Dragons" about St Josemaría Escrivá during the Spanish Civil War. It is very much a film about forgiveness. The line is: "When you forgive, you set someone free – yourself."

An outstanding example of forgiveness, which deeply moved Australia and many people around the world, came on 1 February 2020, when four young children, walking on the footpath of a quiet Sydney street, were killed by an out-of-control vehicle driven at 150 kilometres an hour by a driver under the influence of drugs and alcohol. Three of them were the children of Danny and Leila Abdallah. The following day Leila told the media that she and Danny forgave the driver, that the children belonged to God and he had taken them home. In an interview in Rome in June 2022, when the couple were invited to address the World Meeting of Families, Danny said: "I chose to forgive the offender in obedience to my Father in heaven. If my children were here today, they would say, 'Dad, forgive him.' Forgiveness is more for the forgiver than the forgiven. When you forgive the other person, you start to heal." The following year the couple, along with the mother of the other victim, were instrumental in inaugurating a National Day of Forgiveness, to be celebrated throughout Australia each year on February 1. They also established the "i4give.com foundation" to help the many people who find it difficult to forgive. Through that accident and the parents' response, a whole nation was led to see the importance of forgiving, difficult though it may be at times.

Avoiding prejudices

If we are to love not only those closest to us, but also strangers and even those who have hurt us, it follows that we should love everyone, people of all religions, races, ethnic backgrounds, ages, social class, etc. Absolutely everyone. Again, we are not expected to like everyone, but we can still love them.

If we want a justification for this, it is simply that God our Father loves everyone, and all of us are children of our common Father, God. So, in a real sense, we are all brothers and sisters. This gives us what is sometimes called a spirit of solidarity, of being united in a common family, and therefore feeling responsible for everyone.

Jesus Christ shows us the way in this. He was, of course, Jewish in background, but he loved not only Jews but also the Romans who ruled Israel in his time, healing the servant of a Roman centurion. He loved not only the wealthy, but also the poor. Not only the healthy, but the sick, many of whom he healed. Not only adults, but children, whom he loved dearly. He loved everyone. And he invited us to love others as he has loved us. In the Last Supper he told his disciples: "A new commandment I give to you, that you love one another; even as I have loved you, that you also love one another. By this all men will know that you are my disciples, if you have love for one another" (*John* 13:34-35).

As we read this, we can ask ourselves whether we harbour prejudices against certain classes of people. Many people do. It might be people of certain religions, races, social classes or whatever. If we want to be prepared to face God in the final exam at the end of our life, we should make every effort to rid ourselves of any prejudices we might have.

Putting ourselves out for others

Loving others means putting ourselves out for them too. Jesus Christ did this. Even though he was God, dwelling with the Father and the Holy Spirit from all eternity in heaven, he loved us so much that he became man for us. Then he went even further and died on the cross for us, bringing about our redemption, our reconciliation with God. St John writes in his Gospel that he loved us "to the end" (*John* 13:1).

One of the first things Jesus did in his last meal with the disciples before he died, the Last Supper, in which he celebrated the Jewish feast of Passover, was to wash the disciples' feet. This is quite extraordinary. He was their leader, their teacher, and yet he stooped to perform a role usually reserved for servants: to wash their feet. When he had finished, he told them, and he tells us, "Do you know what I have done to you? You call me Teacher and Lord; and you are right, for so I am. If I then, your Lord and Teacher, have washed your feet, you also ought to wash one another's feet. For I have given you an example, that you also should do as I have done to you" (*John* 13:12-15).

One way of living this is simply to be available to serve those, especially in our own family, who need it. Mothers and fathers do this all the time, serving their children, but even they can usually improve too. And children of all ages can have their regular chores to do, as well as obeying their parents when they ask them to do other jobs. We often have opportunities to serve others in our workplaces too, answering their questions, helping a new staff member to settle in, setting up for a meeting, etc.

Many people live this spirit of service by volunteering in a host of organisations, giving their time to help others without expecting any monetary reward. Their only reward is the great joy of helping someone who needed it. Another way to help others is by making monetary donations to charities which help people in need. There are a host of such charities in every country and they benefit greatly from the generosity of their donors.

In helping others with our time, money or simple concern, we can limit ourselves to doing what is relatively easy or we can go beyond our "comfort zone" to what is a genuine sacrifice. Here again, Christ, gives us the example. He sacrificed his life for us, suffering and dying on the cross. The night before he did that he taught the apostles in the Last Supper, "Greater love has no man than this, that a man lay down his life for his friends" (*John* 15:13).

Normally we are not expected to give our life to help someone, although some people do. We occasionally read in the papers of a person who swam out to rescue someone in distress, only to die in the effort, or of someone who entered a burning building to rescue someone trapped inside and died in the process. These deeds are truly heroic, and not expected of everyone.

But there are many little ways of sacrificing ourselves for others on a daily basis. Parents often get up in the middle of the night to feed or attend to other needs of their little children, losing sleep in the process. They may go to great expense, even borrowing the money, to seek expensive medical treatment overseas or in their own country for a family member. They may stay up all night or spend many hours each day caring for a sick or dying person.

If we love other people in these ways, God will be very merciful to us in the judgment. He will regard what we have done for others as done for him. Jesus himself said so. In describing the final judgment at the end of time, God will say to those who have done much good, "Come, O blessed of my Father, inherit the kingdom prepared for you from the foundation of the world; for I was hungry and you gave me food, I was thirsty and you gave me drink, I was a stranger and you welcomed me, I was naked and you clothed me, I was sick and you visited me, I was in prison and you came to me… Truly, I say to you, as you did it to one of the least of these my brethren, you did it to me… And they will go away … to eternal life" (*Matthew* 25:34-46).

If we fill our life with good deeds, we can look forward to the judgment with confidence. And we should not be discouraged if we see we have not done all we could. Mother Teresa of Calcutta said on one occasion, "We ourselves feel that what we are doing is just a drop in the ocean. But the ocean would be less because of that missing drop." And also, "When we die and it comes time for God to judge us, he will not ask, how many good things have you done in your life? Rather he will ask: How much love did you put into what you did?" These words from a great twentieth-century saint are truly consoling, as well as inspiring.

Having considered these general aspects of love for others, we will now consider particular ways of loving our neighbour, beginning with those in our family. This is the fourth of the commandments given by God to Moses.

7

Honour your father and your mother

In the final exam, God will judge us on how much we have loved both him and those around us. We sometimes refer to the people around us as "our neighbour". But there is a proper order of priority in how we are to love these neighbours. Naturally, and everyone realises this, the first ones we are to love are those closest to us, those in our family. So God, after giving the Jewish people three commandments related to loving God, gave him seven more referring to love for our neighbour, and the first of these regards love within the family: "Honour your father and your mother."

The family is very important in God's plan for humankind. In a sense, the family is the first society in history. From the very beginning and in all civilisations, men and women, moved by their love for each other, united themselves in a life-long relationship that we call marriage, and they expressed their love in a one-flesh union that brought forth children. This was the origin of the family. Families like this have existed in all civilisations.

The welfare of families is vital for the well-being of society. The family could be called the original cell of society, in the sense that society is made up of families, just as the body is made up of cells. When the cells are healthy, so is the body. When the cells are diseased, so is the body. Similarly, when families are healthy, in the sense of being stable, loving and peaceful, so will be the society composed of them.

This makes sense. It is in the family that children learn moral values, that they begin to relate to others and learn to care for the young and the old, the sick and the handicapped, and to exercise freedom and responsibility. They learn to respect their parents and others in authority. They learn to obey the rules of the family and those of their country. As such, the family is a school of social virtues and it contributes greatly to the well-being of society. For this reason, the state should do all in its power to assist families in carrying out their mission, while always recognising and safeguarding the rights of parents to make their own decisions.

Within the family, children were always regarded as a great blessing, and to be left childless a misfortune. Indeed, the first book of the Bible, the book of Genesis, referring to the first couple, Adam and Eve, says: "And God blessed them, and God said to them, 'Be fruitful and multiply, and fill the earth and subdue it'" (*Genesis* 1:28).

When the couple are blessed with children the parents, in addition to loving one another, focus their attention on their children, educating them, teaching them virtues, values, and the various skills they will need in life. They pour out love on them for, after all, the children are the fruit of their love for one another. And the children, naturally, are moved to correspond by loving their parents. In this, we see how natural it is for parents to love their children, and for children to love and honour their parents. In a sense, God didn't need to give us a commandment for this to happen.

Duties of children towards their parents

Since their parents gave the children the gift of life, and they love and sacrifice themselves for them, children naturally have a duty to love and respect their parents. The Old Testament Book of Sirach expresses this duty powerfully: "With all your heart honour your father, and do not forget the birth pangs of your mother. Remember that through your parents you were born; what can you give back to them that equals their gift to you?" (*Sirach* 7:27-28) Children can never give back to their parents what their parents gave them, but they can show them all their love and respect. They do this, among other ways, by being docile and obedient to them.

Nonetheless, it should be clear to both parents and children that there can be situations in which the children need not obey their parents. The first is when the child is convinced in conscience that it would be morally wrong to obey a particular command. For example, if the father asked his son to assist him in stealing a car, the son need not, and should not, obey him.

Second, it is generally accepted that when the child reaches the majority of age, which is usually eighteen, or he leaves home, he is legally an adult and need not obey his parents. Nonetheless, while they are still at home, children should always show great respect to their parents and carry out their reasonable wishes.

Third, children are not obliged to obey their parents in the choice of a profession or a state in life. The parents may have grand designs for what they would like their children to do in life and whom they would like them to marry, but they should realise that this is a matter for the children to decide, not the parents. Naturally, children should always listen to their parents' advice in these matters before choosing the course to follow. Parents, at the same time, should be careful not to exert undue pressure on their children in the choice of a profession or of the decision to marry or not.

What responsibilities do children have towards their parents later in life? Naturally, throughout their life children should continue to love and respect their parents. They should stay in contact with them, show them their concern, seek their advice and give them material and moral support in their old age and in times of illness, loneliness or other difficulties. The Book of Sirach says: "Whoever honours his father will be gladdened by his own children, and when he prays he will be heard... O son, help your father in his old age, and do not grieve him as long as he lives; even if he is lacking in understanding, show forbearance; in all your strength do not despise him..." (*Sirach* 3:5, 12-13).

This assistance to parents in their old age is a good way of repaying the sacrifice the parents made for their children when they were infants and in constant need of care. Moreover, if children see their parents putting themselves out to care for their grandparents in their old age, they in turn will be led to do the same when their parents are in that state.

Duties of parents towards their children

Just as there is nothing so natural as for children to love, honour and obey their parents, so it only natural for parents to fulfil certain duties towards their children. They don't have to be told to do this; they will do it of their own accord. But it is good to remind ourselves of some of these duties nonetheless.

The first and most obvious duty of parents is to love and respect their children, seeing them as truly the gift from God that they are. In a sense, God has entrusted the children to the parents to be cared for on earth until God calls the children to eternal life with him. Naturally, parents should provide for the physical and spiritual needs of their children, including food, shelter, clothing, health care, education, and so on. In general, parents should educate their children in the right use of freedom, so that the children always feel free and they take responsibility for their actions.

Parents live out this responsibility by creating a home where such qualities as tenderness, forgiveness, respect, fidelity and service are the rule. They should teach their children the virtues, including self-denial, sound judgment and self-discipline, which are necessary for true freedom. At the same time, they should not fear to discipline their children, always doing it with love and moderation. In the words of the Book of Sirach: "He who loves his son will not spare the rod... He who disciplines his son will profit by him" (*Sirach* 30:1-2). Naturally, parents teach their children best by giving them good example.

Parents also have the important responsibility of educating their children to believe in God and to worship him in accordance with their belief. If children are taught to pray and to worship God from childhood, they will find it easier to continue to do this all their life. And if the children later marry, they will be moved to bring up their own children to believe in God. Naturally, the best way to educate children in matters of faith is for the parents to practise this faith themselves and give them good example. One day, both parents and children will face God in the judgment and they desperately want to be found worthy.

Rights and duties in civil society

The fourth commandment of God refers not only to the relations between parents and children but more generally to all relations between those in authority and those under them.

What are some of the duties of civil authorities? First, they should exercise their authority in a spirit of service towards those in their care. Also, they should govern according to the principles of justice, not commanding anything that is contrary to the dignity of persons and the natural law. They should facilitate the exercise of freedom and responsibility of all. In apportioning burdens and favours, they should take into account the needs and possibilities of each person in order to foster justice, harmony and peace.

They should respect the fundamental rights of the human person, especially those of families and the disadvantaged. They should respect the political rights attached to citizenship, for example the right to vote, to run for public office, and so on. These rights, which are for the common good, cannot be suspended by public authorities without legitimate and proportionate reasons.

The more prosperous nations are obliged, to the extent that they are able, to welcome people from other countries who come in search of the security and means of livelihood they cannot find in their country of origin. Naturally, political authorities may make the exercise of the right to immigrate subject to various conditions, especially with regard to the immigrants' duties towards their new country. Immigrants, in turn, are obliged to respect with gratitude the material and spiritual heritage of the country that receives them and to obey its laws.

If civil authorities have duties towards those in their care, so too citizens have duties towards those in authority. Citizens have the right, and at times the duty, to exercise their freedom of speech by speaking out on matters that affect the good of the country. At times this may involve expressing their criticism of whatever seems harmful to the dignity of persons and to the good of the community. And, of course, they should fulfil their roles in the life of the community by obeying the laws, paying taxes, exercising the right to vote, and defending their country if the need arises.

8

You shall not kill

We come now to another aspect of love for our neighbour, that of respecting his life as well as our own. The fifth commandment given by God to Moses says: You shall not kill. We all agree that we shouldn't kill an innocent person. We wouldn't want anyone to think it would be quite alright to kill us or a member of our family, and so we shouldn't do that to anyone else.

But really, everything related to the life of others should be seen in the positive context of the love that we owe them. We saw this in chapter five. If we love someone, we wouldn't think of harming or killing them. If there were more love in the world, there would be less violence and killing. And if we truly loved our neighbour, all of our neighbours, we wouldn't even need a commandment to tell us not to kill or harm them.

Actually, the fifth commandment refers to much more than just killing another. It has a wide scope, including taking and harming the life of oneself or of another, and it also includes harming the spiritual life of oneself or another.

The general principle that governs how life is to be treated is that human life is in some way sacred. It was created by God, who created everything in the universe, and God has a love for everything, especially us human beings, who have an intellect and a free will that make us like God. What is more, as we saw in *Dying to Live*, God loved human beings so much that he became man in Jesus Christ so that he could dwell among us on earth and die for us to reconcile us with God after the original sin of the first humans, Adam and Eve. God created every single human being, and he loves every single one. Therefore, we cannot presume to end a life that God has begun. It is up to God to do that, when he thinks the person is ready to face him in the judgment. The book of Job in the Old Testament of the Bible says: "In [God's] hand is the life of every living thing and the breath of all mankind" (*Job* 12:10).

When we hear a commandment like "You shall not kill" we should understand that what the commandment forbids is killing an innocent person. The Bible says as much: "Do not slay the innocent and the righteous" (*Exodus* 23:7). The killing of the innocent can take a variety of forms.

Murder

The first and perhaps most obvious form of killing is *murder*. The Catechism of the Catholic Church is very clear about it: "The deliberate murder of an innocent person is gravely contrary to the dignity of the human being, to the golden rule and to the holiness of the Creator. The law forbidding it is universally valid: it obliges each and everyone, always and everywhere" (*CCC* 2261). Some forms of murder are especially serious because of the natural relationships they break. Among these, the killing of infants, or infanticide, is especially serious since the infant is the most innocent and defenceless of human beings. This includes of course killing deformed and handicapped babies. Other more serious forms of murder are the killing of one's parents, siblings or spouse.

In addition to forbidding direct intentional killing, the fifth commandment also forbids doing anything which could indirectly bring about another's death (cf. *CCC* 2269). Examples are exposing someone to danger of death without grave reason, and refusing to assist a person in danger, with the intention that they will die. It can also include reckless driving of a motor vehicle and driving under the influence of alcohol or drugs, resulting in the death of another.

It goes without saying that, short of actually killing someone, quarrelling and fighting are also sins against the fifth commandment.

Abortion

Another form of killing the innocent is abortion, which is the destruction of the unborn child in the womb. When we consider the sacredness of human life from the moment of conception, it is easy to understand why abortion is so wrong. God loves every human being from the moment it is conceived and for all eternity. In view of this, it is understandable that from the earliest centuries abortion has always been forbidden. Already in the first century, a Christian document known as the *Didache* said: "You shall not kill the embryo by abortion and shall not cause the newborn to perish" (*Didache*, 2, 2).

Not only does abortion end the life of the unborn child, it often does serious harm to the mother and father, who can suffer from post-abortion grief, manifesting itself as depression, emotional instability and so on. But God still loves those who have done wrong and he is always ready to forgive them if they come back to him truly sorry for what they have done. Others too should never condemn those who have had an abortion or who have participated in one. Rather, they should show them every kindness and, where appropriate, help them realise the seriousness of what they have done and ask God to forgive them.

To help people understand the malice of abortion, an interesting exercise would be to ask a group of people how many of them would be in favour of putting to death a man who has raped a woman who, as a result, is now pregnant with a child. Practically no one would raise their hand. If we then asked them how many would be in favour of the woman having an abortion to rid herself of this unwanted pregnancy, many would raise their hand. We could then point out to them how inconsistent it is to be against killing the man who has committed a grave crime and yet to be in favour of killing the innocent child who has done nothing wrong.

One of the most eloquent voices in favour of the unborn child was Mother Teresa of Calcutta. At a National Prayer Breakfast in Washington, DC, on 5 February 1994, she said before President and Mrs Bill Clinton, Vice-President and Mrs Al Gore, and 4,000 others:

> I feel that the greatest destroyer of peace today is abortion, because it is a war against the child, a direct killing of the innocent child, murder by the mother herself. And if we accept that a mother can kill even her own child, how can we tell other people not to kill one another? How do we persuade a woman not to have an abortion? As always, we must persuade her with love and we remind ourselves that love means to be willing to give until it hurts. Jesus gave even his life to love us. So, the mother who is thinking of abortion, should be helped to love, that is, to give until it hurts her plans, or her free time, to respect the life of her child. The father of that child, whoever he is, must also give until it hurts.
>
> By abortion, the mother does not learn to love, but kills even her own child to solve her problems. And, by abortion, that father is told that he does not have to take any responsibility at all for the child he has brought into the world. The father is likely to put other women into the same trouble. So abortion just leads to more abortion. Any country that accepts abortion is not teaching its people to love, but to use any violence to get what they want. This is why the greatest destroyer of love and peace is abortion.

Euthanasia

Euthanasia can be defined as an act or omission which, of itself or by intention, causes death in order to eliminate suffering. That is, euthanasia is the killing of an innocent human being, as is murder, but with the particular motive of eliminating the person's suffering.

Most countries forbid euthanasia and the few that allow it do so only when, under strict conditions, a person has asked voluntarily to be put to death.

It is easy to see how allowing euthanasia goes against the fundamental principle of the equality of all before the law. It establishes two classes of persons: those whose lives are considered worth living and who therefore cannot be put to death, and those whose lives are not considered worth living and who can ask to be put to death. Everyone abhors suicide, but a law allowing euthanasia establishes a class of people who can be assisted to commit suicide. Gradually such laws are extended to more and more people, and the minimum age is gradually reduced as well. All lives are worth living, and this principle should be enshrined in law.

What people who are suffering most want is love and accompaniment, along with whatever can be done to reduce their suffering. So every effort should be made to improve the palliative care available for them. Naturally, certain procedures that prolong the life of the person may be discontinued when it is clear that they are not achieving their aim or that they are burdensome to the person, dangerous or disproportionate to the expected outcome. Here the aim is not to cause death. Rather, one's inability to prevent it is accepted. For example, it is acceptable to disconnect life support when it is clear that without it the person would die anyway of their underlying condition.

Suicide

It is easy to understand why suicide is so wrong, and we all suffer greatly when someone close to us ends their life. Some people might ask what is wrong with suicide. Can't we do with our life whatever we want? No, our life is not something we possess, to be used however we want. Life is a gift from God, to be administered wisely until we are called to give an account of it in the judgment. God is the master of life, and he will decide when it is time for it to end. We are stewards, not owners, of the life God has entrusted to us.

Apart from being an offence against God, who is the master of life, suicide goes against the natural inclination to preserve our life, an inclination written into our nature by God. It is one of our strongest inclinations. In this way suicide is gravely contrary to the just love of self which everyone should have. And it is a grave lack of love for our neighbour, because it affects many people deeply, especially our family and friends.

Although, objectively speaking, suicide is gravely wrong, we can never make judgments about the subjective guilt of persons who have ended their life. Very often psychological or psychotic disturbances, depression, anxiety or fear of hardship, suffering or torture diminish the person's use of reason and of responsibility for their action. We should always pray very much for them, begging God to forgive them and to take them to himself.

Exceptions to the wrongfulness of killing

While it is always wrong to kill an innocent person, there are some circumstances in which a person is not "innocent" and may be put to death. The first of these, as you can imagine, is self-defence, where someone is being attacked by another and may use whatever means are necessary to defend himself or herself, even to the point of killing the assailant as a last resort.

Another circumstance is war. When, in spite of all efforts to prevent it, two countries have gone to war, soldiers may of course use arms to defend themselves and kill the enemy. War is always a scourge in which, in a real sense, there are no winners, and so it should be avoided at all costs. And those with a conscientious objection to fighting in the war, should be allowed to serve in some other capacity so that they are not required to bear arms.

As regards capital punishment, which a diminishing number of countries still have on their books, Popes John Paul II and Benedict XVI called for it to be eliminated altogether. Citing his predecessors, Pope Francis in 2018 declared that, in view of the dignity of the human person, a new understanding of the significance of penalties imposed by the state and the more effective systems of detention now available, "the Church teaches, in the light of the Gospel, that the death penalty is inadmissible because it is an attack on the inviolability and dignity of the person, and she works with determination for its abolition worldwide." This is a welcome development in the Church's teaching. Apart from other considerations, it makes it possible for those wrongfully imprisoned and on death row to prove their innocence and be released, rather than be put to death for a crime they didn't commit.

Giving scandal

As we saw earlier in this chapter, we can offend against the life of another not only by killing or harming them in their body, but also by harming them spiritually, by leading them into sin. This is what is known as scandal, which is traditionally defined as an attitude or behaviour which leads another to commit sin. I suspect we have all done this at one time or another. For example, by encouraging someone to steal or to vandalise property, by encouraging them to read a book or watch a film with inappropriate content, by engaging in sexual activity with someone outside marriage, etc.

Clearly, one of the worst things we can do is lead another person into sin, especially serious sin, which could put them on a path to eternal damnation, to hell. If we have done this, it is very important to be truly sorry. And, if it is still possible, to tell them we are sorry and help them change their ways.

Scandal is especially serious when it is done by people in authority, such as teachers, church leaders or parents, and when those who are led into sin are especially vulnerable, such as children or the handicapped. Christ must have had them in mind when he said: "Whoever causes one of these little ones who believe in me to sin, it would be better for him to have a great millstone fastened round his neck and to be drowned in the depth of the sea" (*Matthew* 18:6).

We should not forget that scandal can also be committed on a broader scale when, for example, governments pass laws that legalise immoral conduct, film makers produce films that display human sexuality in an immoral way, or business leaders encourage fraud or corruption.

Neglecting health

We should look on our health, as on life itself, as a gift entrusted to us by God and so we should take reasonable care of it. Care for our health includes eating a balanced diet, avoiding excesses, taking any prescribed medicines, and getting sufficient rest and exercise. A notable failure in any of these areas would be a violation of the fifth commandment. This is important. After all, if we have good health we can live longer to look after our family and make a greater contribution to society. Failures here could include excessive eating or drinking of alcohol, smoking tobacco excessively and using prohibited drugs. Drunkenness, where the person has lost control of his rationality, is generally a grave sin. Naturally, at the same time we should not foster of a sort of "cult" of the body, by spending excessive time or money on fitness or body image. Moderation in all things.

9

You shall not commit adultery

Sexuality and marriage

Before we look in detail at aspects of morality in the area of sexuality, it is important to understand the relationship between sexuality and marriage. It is really a matter of common sense. We can start from the fundamental calling of everyone to love. In his first encyclical letter, a letter addressed to the whole world, Pope John Paul II explained: "Man cannot live without love. He remains a being that is incomprehensible for himself, his life is senseless, if love is not revealed to him, if he does not encounter love, if he does not experience it and make it his own, if he does not participate intimately in it" (*Redemptor Hominis,* 10). This resonates with all of us. We know how important love is in our own life, both in having received love and in loving others.

In another important document, Pope John Paul wrote: "God created man in his own image and likeness; calling him to existence through love, he called him at the same time for love... Creating the human race in his own image and continually keeping it in being, God inscribed in the humanity of man and woman the vocation, and thus the capacity and responsibility, of love and communion. Love is therefore the fundamental and innate vocation of every human being" (*Familiaris consortio,* 11).

We can all understand this. We were given life through the love of our parents, who loved us dearly, introducing us to what it means to be loved. In the course of our life since then we have experienced the love of others – relatives, friends, colleagues – and we have been able to show love to them as well. Without love, as John Paul II says, life is lacking in something fundamental, it is even senseless, without meaning and direction. Most people will live out their calling to love in marriage, while others will do so in the single state. But all are called to love – to give love and to be loved. Love is our fundamental and innate vocation.

Within this calling to love we see the meaning of sexuality. We were created male and female, and there are approximately equal numbers of men and women on earth. Males and females are complementary to one another in their bodies, their minds and their inclination to love one another and form bonds of communion, friendship and intimacy. This inclination expresses itself in a desire to spend one's whole life together in marriage, and to come together in a one-flesh union of a man and woman through which children come into the world. So, our sexuality is intimately related to our calling to love, to marry and have children. Children are the living expression of the love of their parents, and they participate in that love as soon as they are born.

The virtue of chastity

At the same time, and precisely because of this strong inclination to love another person, to marry and have children, we have the strong urge to seek the pleasure which accompanies the sexual act. It is there so that we will continue the human race. Similarly, we have a strong desire to enjoy the pleasure of eating, so that we will continue in our own personal life. At the same time, we are all aware of a certain disorder in our nature, which affects our ability to control our sexuality and to use it for the purpose for which it is intended.

We are inclined to seek sexual pleasure on our own, with persons to whom we are not married, etc. We see the effects of this in such aspects as the widespread sexual promiscuity among young people, marital infidelity, the growing use of pornography and so on.

As with our other disordered tendencies, like those of laziness, pride, selfishness, etc., we find it easier to control them if we develop the corresponding virtues, or good habits. So in this area too, we will find it easier to use our sexuality properly if we develop the virtue of chastity. As we saw when we considered virtues in chapter three, virtues are good habits which facilitate the doing of good. In the area of sexuality and marriage, we are helped by the virtue of chastity, which moderates the use of sexuality according to right reason. That is, the virtue helps us use our sexuality in keeping with its natural purpose, which is as an expression of love in marriage. We all know how difficult it is to live this virtue at times, to control our strong urge to seek sexual pleasure in the wrong way. We can become almost a slave, addicted to seeking this pleasure. But when we gain the ascendancy over it we become free again. We have a degree of self-mastery, of freedom.

How do we grow in it? The soil in which chastity can grow is, first, watered by prayer; that is, by cultivating a personal relationship of love for God and readiness to do what he is asking of us. And, of course, the first thing he is asking is to be faithful to him, and to ourselves, by saying no to the temptation. Second, the soil is weeded by acts of self-mastery, self-denial in other areas of pleasure, such as food and drink, entertainment, comfort, etc. That doesn't mean we can't enjoy those pleasures, but that we should live them with moderation, not excess. All this helps us to be stronger in resisting temptations and gradually acquiring the self-mastery we want. And we do want it. After all, many marriages break up because of lack of control in this area, with all the devastation divorce brings in its wake.

Offences against chastity

From your experience you can probably guess what most of the offences against chastity are, seeing the harmful consequences that follow from them: adultery, pornography, rape, etc. First though, it is important to know that, as a general rule, external offences against chastity – that is, sins of action as distinct from internal sins of thought or desire – are of themselves serious, or mortal, sins. However, if they are done in ignorance of their seriously disordered nature or without full consent in the will, they may be venial sins or no sin at all. Here we will consider seven of them.

The first one is *lust*, usually defined as disordered desire for sexual pleasure. Sexual pleasure is morally disordered when it is separated from its natural purpose in bringing life into the world through love in marriage. Christ spoke of lust when he said, "You have heard that it was said, 'You shall not commit adultery.' But I say to you that every one who looks at a woman lustfully has already committed adultery with her in his heart" (*Matthew* 5:27-28). We can all be tempted to lust and so we must be on guard to reject the temptations immediately.

The second offence is *masturbation,* understood as the deliberate stimulation of the genital organs in order to derive sexual pleasure. This is probably the easiest sin to commit against chastity, but it can have serious consequences. It turns the person inward towards self, instead of outward towards another, where one's sexuality is used to express love for one's spouse. It can lead to a habit of seeking pleasure and make one dependent on it. This in turn can put pressure on one's spouse in marriage in demanding intimacy when the other spouse may not be able or willing to give it. It can also lead to the use of pornography, which brings with it its own serious consequences. In summary, it is a form of pleasure for pleasure's sake, which is simply hedonism. While in itself it is a serious sin, the culpability can be diminished by such factors as ignorance of its serious nature, immaturity, force of acquired habit, anxiety or depression, and other psychological or social factors.

The third offence against chastity is *fornication*, commonly referred to as sex before marriage. In more general terms it is carnal union between an unmarried man and an unmarried woman. As we have seen, by nature the obvious purpose of sex is as an expression of love in marriage through which new human beings can be born. If a child results from an act of sexual union between unmarried persons, it will often be aborted. Or, if it is brought into the world, it cannot be properly brought up by parents who are not married and living together.

What is more, sex before marriage can have negative consequences for the prospects of a happy marriage in the future. An easy way to understand this is to consider that to have sex with someone with whom you are not married is to get the other person – and yourself – used to having sex with someone to whom they are not married. If you were then to marry that person, and he or she was unfaithful to you, you would have only yourself to blame. After all, you got that person used to having sex with someone to whom they were not married, and now they are doing it to you. Another argument against fornication is that a good-living person wants to marry someone who has their sexuality under control, who is chaste, and not of loose morals. If someone has been having sex outside of marriage, they are not the attractive person others want to marry. As they say, if you want to make a good catch, be a good catch.

The fourth offence is the use of *pornography*. It consists in removing sexual acts from the intimacy of the partners in order to display them deliberately to third parties. It offends against chastity because it perverts the sexual act, the intimate giving of spouses to each other. It causes serious harm to the dignity of all involved, including the actors, distributors and viewers. It immerses all who are involved in the illusion of a fantasy world. As is obvious, it is a serious problem.

One of the worst aspects of pornography is that it divorces the use of sexuality from love, making it merely an object of pleasure for the viewer. It thus portrays men, women, or even children, as mere objects of sexual gratification, as mere bodies, rather than as persons. The availability of pornography on the internet causes grave harm to many persons, as we are all aware. The use of pornography is also a factor in the breakup of many relationships. It is a real scourge.

The fifth offence is *prostitution*, where a person pays another to engage in sexual acts. Like pornography, it reduces the prostitute from being a human person, with the dignity of a member of a family and a child of God, to a mere body, an instrument of sexual pleasure. While it is always seriously sinful to engage in prostitution, the gravity of the offence can be diminished by such factors as poverty, blackmail or social pressure. Sometimes too, the prostitute is forced into this work in a form of modern-day slavery.

The sixth offence is *rape,* the forcible violation of the sexual intimacy of another person. Everyone finds this particularly abhorrent. It deeply wounds the respect, freedom and physical and moral integrity to which everyone has a right. It is always wrong, no matter what the circumstances. Naturally, especially serious is the sexual abuse of a child committed by a family member, a friend of the family, or someone responsible for the care of the child entrusted to them. The effects of the sexual abuse of young people are often life-long, causing serious emotional and mental problems.

Finally, the seventh offence is sexual acts between persons of the same sex, or *homosexual acts*. The Bible, in both the Old and the New Testaments, condemns these acts as gravely immoral. They are contrary to the natural law. They close the sexual act to the gift of life of a new human person.

It is important to understand that, while homosexual acts are gravely immoral, same-sex attraction itself is not sinful. Same-sex attraction refers to an exclusive or predominant sexual attraction toward persons of the same sex. Persons with same-sex attraction have the same dignity as everyone else and they too were redeemed by Christ, who died on the cross for them and desires their eternal salvation. Mother Teresa of Calcutta showed the way for all of us when she was asked in an interview what she thought of gay people. She answered: "You mean beloved children of God?" They must always be accepted with respect and compassion. And, of course, every form of unjust discrimination against them must be avoided.

Openness to life and contraception

By nature, as we have seen, men and women experience a strong attraction for each other and this leads them into the lifelong relationship we call marriage. The spouses express their love for each other in many ways, among them in the sexual act through which children come into the world. This act, as is obvious, is ordered to the birth of children. We see it in animals, where a male and a female come together and from this union offspring are born. In humans this act is not merely something physical, a union of two bodies, but an act of love, a union of two hearts.

The sexual act in marriage is noble and honourable and the pleasure the spouses experience is intended by God. In some sense, it is a foretaste of the joy they will later have in heaven. In this act the spouses express their love and they grow in love for each other. This love in turn bears fruit in children, who are an expression of the love of their parents. We are all aware of the great joy spouses experience when they are blessed with the gift of a child. And, sometimes, the sadness and disappointment when they cannot have children. Indeed, through the marriage act spouses cooperate in a real way with God in the work of creation, giving life to a new human being who, without the parents' love, would not exist. It is an awesome gift – and responsibility. We all give thanks to our parents for the gift of life.

The natural connection between the sexual act and the gift of life was expressed eloquently and simply years ago by an elated young man whose wife had just given birth to their first child. He told me: "Now I understand what sex is for."

In view of this, it is understandable that spouses should be open to the gift of a new life that God may want to give them. Indeed, true love, unconditional love, between the spouses means that their expressions of love are open to life. True love does not admit of any barriers, of any half-giving, of holding anything back. It is unconditional. Pope John Paul II writes:

> In its most profound reality, love is essentially a gift; and conjugal love, while leading the spouses to the reciprocal "knowledge" which makes them "one flesh," does not end with the couple, because it makes them capable of the greatest possible gift, the gift by which they become cooperators with God for giving life to a new human person. Thus, the couple, while giving themselves to one another, give not just themselves but also the reality of children, who are a living reflection of their love, a permanent sign of conjugal unity and a living and inseparable synthesis of their being a father and a mother (*Familiaris Consortio* 14).

Consequently, the use of contraception in any form, including sterilisation, is not an expression of true love. Love is a total giving of the spouses to each other. If they use contraception, the spouses do not give themselves totally but withhold something, putting a barrier between them. In the words of Pope John Paul II:

> Thus, the innate language that expresses the total reciprocal self-giving of husband and wife is overlaid, through contraception, by an objectively contradictory language, namely, that of not giving oneself totally to the other. This leads not only to a positive refusal to be open to life but also to a falsification of the inner truth of conjugal love, which is called upon to give itself in personal totality" (*Familiaris Consortio* 32).

Lest you think that the wrongfulness of the use of contraception is a modern teaching, I can assure you that it is not. It is very ancient.

As early as the year 191 AD, Clement of Alexandria wrote that "to have coitus other than to procreate children is to do injury to nature" (*The Instructor of Children* 2:10, 91, 2). A few years later, in 225 St Hippolytus decried the fact that certain women "use drugs of sterility or bind themselves tightly in order to expel a foetus which has already been engendered" (*Refutation of All Heresies 9:12*).

In the year 375 Epiphanius of Salamis also condemned the use of means to prevent conception. Speaking of certain people, he wrote: "They exercise genital acts, yet prevent the conceiving of children. Not in order to produce offspring, but to satisfy lust, are they eager for corruption" (*Medicine Chest Against Heresies 26:5, 2*).

In 391 Saint John Chrysostom spoke strongly against spouses who prevented the conception of children: "Why do you sow where the field is eager to destroy the fruit, where there are medicines of sterility, where there is murder before birth? You do not even let a harlot remain only a harlot, but you make her a murderess as well... Indeed, it is something worse than murder, and I do not know what to call it; for she does not kill what is formed but prevents its formation..." (*Homilies on Romans* 24).

To quote one more ancient text from a well-known writer, St Augustine in 419 was scathing in his criticism of spouses who engaged in marital intercourse while preventing conception: "I am supposing, then, although you are not lying [with your wife] for the sake of procreating offspring, you are not for the sake of lust obstructing their procreation by an evil prayer or an evil deed. Those who do this, although they are called husband and wife, are not; nor do they retain any reality of marriage, but with a respectable name cover a shame. Sometimes this lustful cruelty, or cruel lust, comes to this, that they even procure poisons of sterility... Assuredly if both husband and wife are like this, they are not married, and if they were like this from the beginning, they come together not joined in matrimony but in seduction. If both are not like this, I dare to say that either the wife is in a fashion the harlot of her husband or he is an adulterer with his own wife" (*Marriage and Concupiscence 1:15, 17*). Strong words indeed.

So, from the earliest centuries the use of contraception was looked upon as contrary to the very purpose of marriage. Indeed, all Christian denominations taught this until 1930, when the Lambeth conference of the Anglican church broke ranks and allowed the use of contraception. At the end of that year, by way of reaffirming the Catholic Church's centuries-old stand on the issue, Pope Pius XI wrote the Encyclical letter *Casti connubii*. After mentioning some of the reasons why couples may not want to have children, he wrote that the use of contraception goes against nature itself: "But no reason whatever, even the gravest, can make what is intrinsically against nature become conformable with nature and morally good. The conjugal act is of its very nature designed for the procreation of offspring; and therefore those who in performing it deliberately deprive it of its natural power and efficacy, act against nature and do something which is shameful and intrinsically immoral" (*CC* 54). He went on to say that "any use of matrimony whatsoever in the exercise of which the act is deprived, by human interference, of its natural power to procreate life, is an offence against the law of God and of nature, and that those who commit it are guilty of grave sin" (*CC* 56).

In 1968 Pope Paul VI repeated this teaching in his Encyclical *Humanae vitae*. After saying that abortion and sterilisation are excluded as lawful ways of regulating birth he added: "Similarly excluded is every action which, either in anticipation of the conjugal act, or in its accomplishment, or in the development of its natural consequences, proposes, whether as an end or as a means, to render procreation impossible" (*HV* 14).

This teaching may sound strange and even harsh to many people these days. After all, contraception is readily available and widely used. But when you consider it in the light of the meaning of love, sexuality and marriage, it makes sense. Eminent sense. The brilliant British journalist Malcolm Muggeridge, an avowed atheist who became a Catholic at the age of 79, thought so too. In a radio interview in 1985 he said:

> It was *Humanae vitae* more than anything else which made me feel that I must belong to the one Church that could have the extraordinary insight and courage to produce that as an encyclical, knowing that it would be absolutely torn to pieces, that its doctrine was almost a kind of blasphemy in the eyes of the idiotic society we live in. This was one of the things that made me feel that I must be counted up with those who stand firm, because they are alone... There is nobody else that has done this, you see, there is not another voice that has been raised in any denomination, except some ultra-Protestant ones, to take the same position.

It is helpful to know that most oral contraceptive pills and Intra-Uterine Devices (IUDs) have as one of their mechanisms to prevent pregnancy an abortifacient effect, so that makes them unacceptable on that ground as well.

Naturally, if there are serious reasons why a couple should not have another child for the time being or even indefinitely, they can make use of their marriage only during the infertile periods of the wife through what is called natural family planning. Here the marriage act is of itself open to life even though the couple know that it is highly unlikely that it will result in the conception of a baby. And always the couple are open to receive a new child, should God send them one. There are various methods of natural family planning and in general they can be very effective. Many couples who used contraception for some time and found the side effects unpleasant or even dangerous to their health, have gone over to natural family planning and found it much more suitable. Naturally, this method requires the cooperation of husband and wife in abstaining from marital relations for some days each month, but this in turn can serve to strengthen the marriage. Many couples have found this to be the case.

Offences against the dignity of marriage

In addition to offences against chastity and openness to life, there are also offences against marriage itself, understood in its normal sense as the union of a man and woman to the exclusion of all others, voluntarily entered into for life. God blesses marriage and he wants it to be stable and loving. Everyone is better off, including the spouses, the children and the whole of society, when marriage is stable and strong. So, it is understandable that whatever can endanger the stability of marriage is seriously harmful to all concerned. Here we will consider three principal offences against marriage: adultery, divorce, and polygamy.

Adultery

The sixth commandment of God states: "You shall not commit adultery". By adultery we understand, of course, sexual relations between two persons of whom at least one is married to someone else. Everyone agrees that adultery is a serious offence against marriage. In marrying, the spouses committed themselves to remain faithful to each other all their lives and adultery is a violation of that promise. It is an offence not only against chastity, but also against justice and charity. A person who commits adultery fails in his or her commitment to their spouse to remain faithful. The spouses have a right to the fidelity of their partner and adultery violates that right, so it is an offence against justice. And it is obviously an offence against charity, since it shows a great lack a love for one's spouse.

It is not always easy to be faithful to one's spouse, especially if the marriage has become "stale" and a more loving person enters one's life. But then the commitment to fidelity made in the marriage ceremony should be recalled, along with the knowledge of the great harm that adultery can cause, not only to one's spouse but also to their children. And perhaps too to the spouse and family of the other person involved, if he or she is also married. If a couple's love has grown cold, they should make an effort to warm it up by little acts of kindness: spending more time talking together, going out on dates, showing the other that they really love them. And, of course, they should get marriage counselling. By putting more love into the relationship they can often come back to the love they had at the beginning, to the great joy of everyone. Instead of thinking how nice it would be to be married to someone else, they should work on their own marriage. As they say, if the grass is greener on the other side of the fence, water your grass!

Divorce

The breakup of a marriage, as we have seen, causes great harm to the spouses, to their children and to the whole of society. The spouses suffer from the lack of love they expected from their spouse, from the breakup of their life project and the shattering of their dreams. The children suffer greatly, whether they are infants, adolescents or even married themselves. What is more, surveys show that children of divorced parents are more likely to get divorced themselves. And society suffers. We see this in schools, where children of divorced parents can be troubled and disruptive; in workplaces, where a divorced person takes out their own distress on their colleagues; and even on the roads where road rage is more common.

Jesus Christ was very clear on the evil of divorce: "Every one who divorces his wife and marries another commits adultery, and he who marries a woman divorced from her husband commits adultery" (*Luke* 16:18). Naturally, if there are serious reasons why a couple should not remain together they are always free to separate, but they should not presume to break the marriage bond through civil divorce. If obtaining a civil divorce is necessary to secure the protection of the law as regards property, maintenance or the custody of children, this is of course acceptable.

Polygamy

In some cultures and religions, polygamy is allowed. In polygamy, of course, a man has more than one wife. It is clear, nonetheless, that nature does not allow polygamy to be widespread since there are approximately equal numbers of men and women in the world and polygamy would leave many men without wives. One can also consider that polygamy is contrary to the equal personal dignity of men and women, who in marriage give themselves with a love that is total and therefore exclusive. In polygamy, the husband has several wives but the wives have to share one husband.

9

You shall not steal

As we have seen, each of the last seven commandments given by God to the Jewish people through Moses relates to a different good of our neighbour. We come now to the seventh commandment, "You shall not steal", which relates to our neighbour's property. It is a commandment which people of all countries and religions accept. All countries have laws forbidding stealing with their corresponding punishments for those who break the law. It is only natural. Stealing another's property is wrong. We wouldn't want anyone to steal our property and so we shouldn't steal anyone else's. Actually, the commandment refers to a wide range of aspects of our relations with others as regards property. They come under the general heading of justice.

Justice

But what is justice? It is traditionally defined as the virtue which inclines us to give to each one his due. That is, to give to others what is owed to them. To give them what they are owed in justice is the minimum we must do for them,. For example, we must pay our workers the wage we have agreed upon, we must return property we have borrowed from them, we must work hard to give our employer the work we have agreed to do, and so on. Later in this chapter we will consider a good number of these duties.

But once we have lived justice, we shouldn't stop there. We

should go on to live the many aspects of charity we have already considered. We should treat others kindly, be generous with our time in helping them when they are in need, give donations to individuals and charities... Charity goes beyond justice and gives to others what is not strictly owed to them but what will help them and what they will appreciate very much, precisely because it was not owed to them. When we face God in the judgment, the final exam, we will naturally be held to account for how we have lived justice, but also for how we have lived charity.

The duties of justice with regard to property are situated within the scope of two fundamental principles. The first is what is known as the *universal destination of the world's goods*. It means simply that God intended the world's goods – the air, the water, natural resources, food, etc. – to be available for all human beings, not just for the wealthy, the powerful. That is, we have a duty to ensure that everyone has at least the basics they need to survive. The second principle is the *right to private property*. In order to ensure that each person has access to what he needs for himself and for those in his care, it is fitting that people be able to own property. The ownership of property not only gives security and the ability to provide for the future, it also enhances the sense of freedom and responsibility, and indeed the dignity, of persons.

There is an order of priority between these two principles: the universal destination of goods takes precedence over the right to private property. So, if there are people who are going without the basic necessities of life, those with private property must come to their assistance so that everyone has what he needs. We will see examples of this later.

Respect for the property of others

The principal sin against the seventh commandment is stealing, or theft. It is defined as taking another's property against the reasonable will of the owner. We can understand what is wrong with theft by applying the golden rule: Do to others as you would have them do to you. Or don't do to others what you would not have them do to you. Just as we would not want anyone to steal our goods, it is a matter of justice that we should not steal the goods of anyone else. Moreover, in every country stealing is a crime punishable by law.

However, it is good to know that there are two situations in which taking the property of another is not stealing. Remember that we defined stealing as taking another's property against the reasonable will of the owner. The first situation in which taking another's property would not be stealing is if the consent of the owner can be presumed. And yes, there are circumstances in which we can presume that the owner would be happy for us to take his property. For example, if our next-door neighbour has an apple tree and every year he gives us some apples, and in a given year he is away when the apples are ripe, we can presume that he would be happy for us to take some of his apples as usual. This would not be stealing, since we can presume the consent of the owner.

The second situation is if refusal to give another some of one's property is contrary to reason and the universal destination of goods. This is the case of what is called "obvious and urgent necessity". Here, if someone is lacking immediate, essential goods, such as food or clothing and, after repeated asking, no one will give him anything, he can take from another what he needs to survive. This is not stealing. Since God intended the world's goods for the use of all, if someone is going hungry and no one will give him anything, he can take from another what he needs to relieve his immediate needs – eggs, a chicken, some bread or fruit – without being guilty of the sin of stealing. Obviously, this situation would occur very rarely.

But stealing is not only taking another's property without their consent. There are many other ways to offend against justice. They include deliberate keeping of goods lent or of objects lost without a reasonable effort to find the owner, business fraud, and paying unjust wages. Likewise, corruption, taking for one's own use the common goods of one's workplace, work poorly done, habitually arriving late for work or leaving early, spending excessive time at work on one's personal affairs, tax evasion, forgery of cheques and invoices… The list goes on.

Another offence is wilfully damaging the property of another, or vandalism. This can include scratching or denting another's parked car by careless driving and not leaving a note with one's contact details. This is just a sample of the many possible sins against the seventh commandment.

Restitution

Obviously, as with all sins, if we have violated the seventh commandment, we must be sincerely sorry for what we have done. But that is not all. An important principle here is that if we have stolen or damaged another's property, we are morally obliged to make restitution for the harm caused. This would involve returning the stolen goods to the owner or paying for them, as well as paying for any losses the owner suffered as a result of not having the goods in his possession. For example, if someone damaged a taxi, he would be liable to pay, not only for the cost of the repairs, but also for the amount of money the taxi driver would have earned while his car was off the road. If many years have passed and the person cannot remember from whom items were stolen, it is sufficient to make restitution by giving extra donations to charitable causes.

You may be wondering how serious the sin of stealing is. Is it a venial or a mortal sin? The answer depends on the amount of harm caused to the owner. Some thefts will be only a venial sin and some clearly mortal. A traditional "rule of thumb" is that the theft of the equivalent of a day's wages of a person would constitute a mortal sin. But it is not a matter of drawing lines between venial and mortal sins. We should resolve not to steal at all.

How about gambling? Is it a sin? The answer is that gambling, whether playing games of chance or betting, is not in itself contrary to justice. However, it can become morally unacceptable if it deprives someone of what is necessary to provide for his needs and those of others in his care. Also, as we are all aware, gambling can become an addiction and cause serious harm to the individual and his family, even leading to the breakup of a marriage. It is therefore important to know when to stop gambling so that it does not lead to excessive losses or become an entrenched habit. And we should encourage others to seek professional help if they have this problem.

Care for the environment

Another justice issue is care for the environment. Yes, a justice issue. Creation, with its water, air, resources, plants and animals, is destined by God for the common good of all generations, present and future. So it is a matter of justice to care for it, not only with respect to God but also with respect to our fellow human beings of the present and future generations. Here we must avoid two extremes. On one hand, considering nature a taboo and not touching it, when it was intended by God to be used for the benefit of mankind. On the other, wantonly abusing it, destroying it unnecessarily. In a word, man is a steward of creation on behalf of the Creator, not the master of it.

10

You shall not bear false witness

As we continue to consider moral issues with respect to the various goods of our neighbour, we come to the eighth commandment: "You shall not bear false witness against your neighbour". It refers to two great goods of our neighbour: his right to the truth and his good name. Once again, this commandment is readily understood and accepted by people of all faiths and of none. In simple terms, the first good forbids telling lies and the second forbids harming our neighbour's reputation.

Respect for the truth

Before we delve into the issue of telling lies, we should consider the important virtue of truthfulness, of living in the truth. After all, moral life is not only about avoiding doing the wrong thing. It is about striving always to do the right thing. A good starting point for living in the truth is to remember that God is truth. He knows everything, for he created everything, and everything he teaches is true. As they say, God can neither deceive nor be deceived. When we meet him in the judgment, we will see that he knows everything, including the truth about us, about how we have lived, about everything we have done. This thought moves us to live in the truth ourselves, to practise the virtue of truthfulness, to be honest with ourselves and others.

It is easy to deceive ourselves. To pretend, for example, that there is nothing wrong with something we have done, when deep down we know very well there is something wrong with it. And it is fairly easy to deceive others, to tell a lie, for example, that leads someone else astray. But once again, we cannot deceive God. He knows everything we do and he will judge us by the objective standard of the natural law, which demands that we live in the truth.

What is more, by our very nature we seek truth. We see this in children, who are always asking questions: Why is the sky blue? Where do babies come from? And so on. We adults seek answers to more fundamental questions. Where did the universe come from? Has it always been here or did it have a beginning? Is there life after death. Is there a God? We seek the truth and so does everyone else, so it is only natural that we should always strive to learn more and more, and to communicate the truth of what we have learned to others.

To seek the truth, to hold to the truth and to communicate the truth are all aspects of the virtue of truthfulness, which could be defined as the virtue which consists in showing oneself truthful in deeds and in words, and in guarding against deceitfulness and hypocrisy. The virtue is also called sincerity or candour. As we have seen, this virtue is absolutely fundamental for our dealings with others and for the well-being of society. An easy way to understand the evil of lying is to imagine what would happen if there were nothing wrong with telling lies, and as a result many people told them. Then we couldn't trust anyone and society would break down. We couldn't deposit money in the bank because we couldn't be sure the bank would give it back. You see what I mean. St Thomas Aquinas puts it bluntly: "Men could not live with one another if there were not mutual confidence that they were being truthful to one another" (*Summa Theologiae* II-II, 109, 3 *ad* 1).

What is more, the virtue of truthfulness is related to justice, in the sense that it gives to another what is his due. People have a right to know that what is communicated to them is true. This does not mean, naturally, that we are obliged to tell everyone the whole truth. We are all aware of situations in which it is not appropriate to tell someone the whole truth about a particular matter. For example, parents need not reveal to their children certain aspects of their own relationship or of their financial situation. The solution in these cases is not to tell lies, but simply to remain silent about certain matters. But, as always, everything we say should be true.

Offences against the truth

The most obvious offence against the truth is the lie, which St Augustine defines as "speaking a falsehood with the intention of deceiving" (*De mendacio* 4, 5). Of great importance is the phrase "with the intention of deceiving." Thus, for example, if someone says sincerely that today is Tuesday when in fact it is Wednesday, he is telling an untruth but not a lie. Only when a person knowingly tells an untruth with the intention of deceiving is it a lie. In view of this, when someone says something which is clearly untrue, we must be careful not to accuse him of lying, for he may sincerely believe he is telling the truth. Jesus Christ denounces lying as the work of the devil: "You are of your father the devil... there is no truth in him. When he lies, he speaks according to his own nature, for he is a liar and the father of lies" (*John* 8:44).

Since the purpose of speech is to communicate the truth to others, the deliberate intention of leading another into error by saying things contrary to the truth constitutes an offence against both justice and charity. In a sense, a lie does real violence to the other person, since it affects his ability to know, which is a condition of every judgment and decision he must make.

How serious is the sin of lying? The answer is that the gravity of a lie is measured against the nature of the truth it deforms, the circumstances, the intentions of the one who lies, and especially the harm caused to the other person. In general, a lie in itself, insofar as it is contrary to truthfulness, is a lesser sin, but it becomes grave when it does serious injury to the virtues of justice and charity. Only when it causes grave harm to another would a lie be a mortal sin.

As we all know, especially serious is perjury, telling a lie under oath in court, or bearing false witness. Perjury is especially serious because it is a lie made under oath, thus calling upon God to bear witness to it. And also, because it can contribute to the conviction of someone who is innocent, or the acquittal of someone who is guilty, resulting in a grave injustice.

Offences against the reputation of another

Bearing false witness against our neighbour also includes offences which harm our neighbour's reputation. We all know that our reputation in the eyes of others is very important to us. It affects our dealings with others and our ability to function well in society. Without a good reputation people will not trust us and we will find it difficult to get a job or to enter into meaningful relationships. Therefore, it is very important to respect our neighbour's reputation, just as we expect others to respect ours. St Thomas Aquinas is very clear on this: "It is a serious matter to take away the good esteem of another, because among man's temporal possessions nothing is more precious than his good name; if he lacks this, he is prevented from doing many good things. Therefore, it is said: 'Take care of your good name; for this will be a more lasting possession of yours than a thousand valuable and precious treasures'" (*Summa Theologiae* II, II, q. 73, a. 2; *Ecclesiasticus* 41:15).

There are three principal offences against the reputation of our neighbour: rash judgment, detraction and slander.

Rash judgment

The first sin, rash judgment, is a judgment which remains in our mind and consists in assuming as true, without sufficient reason, the moral fault of another person. For example, we may think that some member of our family has taken our wallet, when in fact we have simply left it in the car. Or we may judge that, because someone is late for an appointment, he is at home watching the end of a television program, when it fact he has been held up in a traffic jam.

While we can judge another's external behaviour – for example, that someone arrived late for work three days in a row – we can never presume to judge why they did it. It would be a rash judgment to conclude that they were lazy and trying to cheat the employer, when in fact their wife may have been in hospital and they had to drive the children to school. Rash judgment consists precisely in making a judgment of the intentions or motives of others without sufficient foundation. Therefore, when we do not know the motives, in order to avoid sinning by rash judgment we should endeavour, as a general rule, to interpret the other's conduct in a favourable way, giving them the benefit of the doubt. After all, that is how we would like others to treat us.

Christ himself was very clear on this: "Judge not, that you be not judged. For with the judgment you pronounce you will be judged, and the measure you give will be the measure you get" (*Matthew* 7:1-2).

When all is said and done, God alone is the supreme judge, and he knows what everyone has done and why they did it. One day he will be our judge too. We desperately want him to judge us fairly, so we too should make an effort to judge others fairly.

Detraction

The second sin, detraction, consists in disclosing, without good reason, another's faults and failings to persons who did not know them. Here the other person has in fact done something wrong, but we reveal this fault to others without a sufficient reason. For example, we may be aware that someone is addicted to gambling or to alcohol, but we have no right to reveal this to others, for that would be to blacken the person's reputation. Just as we would not want others to blacken our reputation in this way, so we must avoid doing so to them. The most common form of detraction is what is known as gossip, where people pass on to others negative aspects of someone's life. When others want to pass on gossip, we should show no interest and, if possible, say something good about the person.

Are there circumstances in which it would be justifiable to pass on this information? Yes, but only when it is necessary for the good of the person with the fault, for the common good or for the good of some other innocent person. For example, if we know that a young person has a habit of using drugs or is contemplating suicide, we could disclose this to their parents or to someone else in a position to help them. Or, if we know that someone running for public office has a history of dishonesty, we could make this fact known. In general, there will be few cases in which we can reveal the hidden faults of others.

Slander

The third sin against the good name of our neighbour is slander, sometimes called calumny. It consists in telling lies that damage another's reputation. It is obvious that slander is even worse than detraction since it involves a lie that damages our neighbour's reputation. We all know how we would feel if someone told lies about us, and so we should be careful to avoid doing so to others.

What is so harmful about slander is that it is practically impossible to restore a person's good name once it has been damaged. Even though the person who told the lie apologises publicly and defends the good name of the other, people will always harbour suspicions that the person may actually be guilty of the fault.

Because everyone has a right to a good name, sins against the good name of another are a violation of justice as well as of charity. And, as with other sins against justice, there is an obligation to do whatever we can to make restitution for the harm caused by detraction and slander, but it is usually almost impossible to restore the person's good reputation. "The mud sticks", as they say. To illustrate this point, the sixteenth-century priest St Philip Neri is said to have told a woman who was known for spreading gossip to take a feather pillow to the top of the church bell tower, cut it open, and let the wind blow the feathers away. When she had done this, he asked her to go back and collect all the feathers that, by now, had been scattered throughout the town. This, of course, she would have found impossible to do. He wanted to show her that it would be no easier to go around to all the people who had heard the gossip and undo the damage it had caused than to collect all the feathers.

To avoid falling into these offences, it is important to avoid curiosity about others' lives, to show a dislike for gossip, to be very careful in talking about others, saying only positive things about them, and to listen to both sides before making a judgment about others.

Revealing secrets

Another way of damaging other people's reputation is to reveal their secrets without good reason. We may come to know certain sensitive things through observing them ourselves, through friends who reveal them to us or through our professional work, for example in the case of doctors, counsellors, lawyers, accountants, politicians, and so on. In all these cases we are obliged not to reveal confidential information if revealing it could harm another in any way.

Nonetheless, there can be circumstances in which secrets may be revealed for a proportionate reason. As a general rule, this may be done only in exceptional circumstances, where keeping the secret is bound to cause very grave harm to the one who confided it, to the one who received it or to a third party, and where the harm can be avoided only by divulging the truth. For example, as we saw before, if someone confided to us that they were taking drugs, contemplating suicide or setting fire to someone's house, we could reveal this to someone who was in a position to prevent this from happening.

But otherwise, secrets are to be kept. This is not always easy, because we all like to pass on to others the juicy things we have heard. I remember reading in a novel how this tendency can lead to the content of secrets becoming known by everyone. It begins with someone hearing a secret and feeling the need to share it with someone, but only with someone who they are sure will not pass it on to anyone else. So they tell them. They, in turn, feel the need to share it, but only with someone who will not pass it on to anyone else. And this person in turn does the same. And soon, everyone knows. So much for secrets.

12

You shall not covet

So far we have been considering the commandments of God which relate to external actions with respect to our neighbours' various goods: goods like family, marriage, life, property, reputation, etc. We come now to the last two commandments, the ninth and tenth, which forbid internal sins, disordered thoughts against our neighbour's spouse and property. They relate respectively to the subject matter of the sixth and seventh commandments. The ninth, "You shall not covet your neighbour's wife", refers to thoughts and desires against marriage and chastity, and the tenth, "You shall not covet your neighbour's goods", to thoughts and desires against the property of others.

You might be inclined to ask why God would give separate commandments which are so closely related to those other two commandments. Wouldn't the prohibition of committing adultery, for example, include desires of adultery too? Of course it would. The answer must be simply that, since marriage and property are such fundamental goods in human life, God wanted to emphasise their importance by forbidding even thoughts and desires against them.

You shall not covet your neighbour's wife

We can begin with the ninth commandment, about coveting our neighbour's wife. The word "covet", by the way, means to desire in a disordered way. As we saw when we studied the sixth commandment,

Jesus Christ himself spoke of these disordered lustful desires: "You have heard that it was said, 'You shall not commit adultery.' But I say to you that every one who looks at a woman lustfully has already committed adultery with her in his heart" (*Matthew* 5:27-28).

So, the ninth commandment is calling us to live what we might call purity of heart, so that our affections and desires are always properly ordered. What do we mean by the heart, in this sense? In common language we often refer to the heart as the seat of moral personality. For example, we read in the Gospel of Matthew: "Out of the heart come evil thoughts, murder, adultery, fornication ..." (*Matthew* 15:19). The struggle against the wayward desires of the flesh, therefore, entails purifying the heart and practising temperance.

Jesus Christ calls us to purity of heart when he gives us what have come to be called the Beatitudes, from the Latin word for blessed. One of these Beatitudes is, "Blessed are the pure in heart, for they shall see God" (*Matthew* 5:8). To be pure in heart means to have our thoughts and desires ordered to their true good, to God and the true good of man, not to what is sinful and offensive to God. Purity of heart is very important in moral life. If we have our heart oriented toward God and his will, then it is free to love what is good and noble in life, and we can more readily see God, both in this life and in the next. We see our neighbour, for example, not just as a body and an object of sexual desire, but as a person, a fellow human being, a son or daughter of God. And we will more readily respect them and treat them accordingly. What a great difference there is between someone with purity of heart, who looks on his neighbour as a child of God, and someone who looks on the person's body with lust, as an object of pleasure.

Purity of heart is very much associated with the virtue of modesty. We all have an understanding of modesty. A modest person dresses and acts with dignity, with modesty, not in a lewd, impure manner which appeals to the lustful desires of others. The Catechism of the Catholic Church gives a beautiful explanation of the role of modesty: "Modesty protects the mystery of persons and their love. It encourages patience and moderation in loving relationships; it requires that the conditions for the definitive giving and commitment of man and woman to one another be fulfilled. Modesty is decency. It inspires one's choice of clothing. It keeps silence or reserve where there is evident risk of unhealthy curiosity. It is discreet" (*CCC* 2522).

What we see in all this is the importance of looking on others as human persons with all their dignity, not seeing them in a lustful, sensual way. What does the ninth commandment forbid? It is traditionally taught that there are three types of internal sins against chastity: taking pleasure in past sins, desire of future unchaste acts, and taking pleasure in imaginary unchaste acts. With all of them it is important to remember that unchaste thoughts, desires, memories or imaginations on their own are not sinful. It is only when the will consents to them, deliberately taking pleasure in them, that they become sinful.

You shall not covet your neighbour's goods

We have now come to the last of the commandments, the tenth, where we are told not to covet our neighbour's goods, not to desire them in a disordered way. Amongst other things, the commandment forbids greed, or avarice, which is a disordered desire for material things, which can lead to such offences as stealing and fraud. Greed is a sort of idolatry, a worshipping of money and material goods rather than worshipping their creator. A sixteenth-century Church document, the *Roman Catechism*, explains it graphically, quoting the Old Testament book of Sirach:

> When the Law says, "You shall not covet," these words mean that we should banish our desires for whatever does not belong to us. Our thirst for another's goods is immense, infinite, never quenched. Thus it is written: "He who loves money never has

money enough" (*Roman Catechism,* III, 37; cf. *Sirach* 5:8).

We know the truth of the statement that whoever loves money never has money enough. We see how some very wealthy people are never satisfied with what they have and their greed leads them to invent dishonest schemes to make even more money, until they finally get caught and go to jail.

The tenth commandment also forbids envy of others' goods, or sadness at the sight of another's goods and the immoderate desire to acquire them for oneself, even unjustly. It can lead to the worst forms of injustice, including stealing the goods or even killing the owner to obtain his property.

As we saw in Chapter 3, envy, like greed, is one of the seven deadly or capital sins. The early Church writers wrote powerfully about it. For example, St Augustine saw envy as "the diabolical sin" (*De catechizandis rudibus* 4, 8), and St Gregory the Great wrote: "From envy are born hatred, detraction, calumny, joy caused by the misfortune of a neighbour, and displeasure caused by his prosperity" (*Moralia in Job* 31, 45).

What can we do to overcome the tendency to envy and greed? In the first place we should make a constant effort to grow in our love for God, who is the infinite good and who alone can satisfy the longings of our heart. We recall the well-known words of St Augustine: "You have made us for yourself, and our heart is restless until it rests in you" (*Confessions.* 1, 1, 1). The more we love God, the less we will be concerned about the things of this world. At the same time, we should make an effort to be more detached from material things, following Christ's advice: "Therefore do not be anxious, saying, 'What shall we eat?' or 'What shall we drink?' or 'What shall we wear?' For the Gentiles seek all these things; and your heavenly Father knows that you need them all. But seek first his kingdom and his righteousness, and all these things shall be yours as well" (*Matthew* 6:31-33). Jesus sums it up in the Beatitudes: "Blessed are the poor in spirit, for theirs is the Kingdom of Heaven" (*Matthew* 5:3).

We can also strive to be generous with our wealth, no matter how much or little we may have. There are many people in this world who go without, even in our own countries, and we can donate money to the various charities which help them. In so doing, we are storing up treasure in heaven and serving Jesus Christ himself, who said: "I was hungry and you gave me food, I was thirsty and you gave me drink, I was a stranger and you welcomed me, I was naked and you clothed me" (*Matthew* 25: 35-36).

Just as we were made by God, in his image and likeness, so we are called to be with God forever in heaven. If we are detached from the things of this world, we will have our heart more in God and less in goods. We will have a greater desire to see God and be with him for all eternity in heaven. We will be very well prepared to meet God in the judgment and pass the final exam.

At this point you might be looking back at all we have seen regarding the ten commandments of God and thinking: "This is heavy stuff. So much to think about. So much we have to do and so much to avoid. Thank God there are only ten!" I agree, but when you think about it, all of what we have studied is only natural, only obvious. The commandments, after all, are statements of the natural law, moral requirements of our human nature, which we all have in common. They are really just common sense. And, for our consolation, as I once heard purportedly coming from a Protestant minister, God has told us only a handful of things we can't do. All the rest we are free to do. A nice way to look at it.

13

The final exam

And so we come to the final exam. Truly the final exam. The last one we will ever take. And the most important. We have to pass this one or be lost forever. The purpose of this book has been to prepare you for this exam, the judgment, so that you will know what to expect and you can live your life accordingly. Really, if you try to live in accordance with what you have read in the preceding pages, you will be well prepared. This doesn't mean you won't fail along the way and do the wrong thing. We all do. But as long as you are truly sorry for your failings, God will forgive you. He always does. He is ever rich in mercy. Really, God *is* mercy.

In this last chapter we will look at some aspects of what we can expect in the judgment, so that there are no surprises when we get there.

We must be sorry for our sins

As we saw in the last chapter of *Dying to Live*, sorrow for our sins is an absolutely fundamental condition for being forgiven by God, who is always merciful and wants us to be with him for all eternity in heaven. Our sorrow must be genuine, with a true conversion of heart. This implies that we are resolved to do all we can to avoid falling into those same offences again, even though we know that, in our weakness, we may very well fall again. But at least we are determined to try. Sorrow is not simply saying some sorrowful words with no real intention to try to improve.

We can understand this if we consider how earthly parents will always forgive their children who have done the wrong thing but come back sincerely sorry for what they have done. And they are understanding when, after the children say they are sorry, they go back and do the same thing again. And again. After all, parents know themselves and they know how often they have been sorry for something but have gone out and done it again. Mind you, it is not that we are creating God in our own image and likeness, making him out to be like us but only a lot better. He made us in *his* image and likeness and he shares with us a heart capable of loving and forgiving. Again and again.

I recently read a beautiful story of forgiveness involving a man named Joaquin who was in the maximum security area of an Argentinian prison, having been convicted of murder. One day he got up the courage to do something he had wanted to do for years. "I left a family without a father", he said. "I've been carrying that on my back for many years and it tears me up inside. I want to call that family and ask for their forgiveness." Through a friend, he got in touch with the family and the widow agreed to take his call. His hands were shaking when he dialled the number. When the widow answered, he introduced himself and apologised profusely for what he had done. She replied: "I thank you for calling me. I cannot judge you. I hope you recover so that this does not happen to others. Don't cry. God hears and sees that humbled heart. God forgave you. That should give you peace of mind, even if you have to serve a sentence here on earth. You have repented. All that remains is that when you get out, you keep seeking him with all your heart and don't go back to the old days." Joaquin cried all that night. He was finally freed from a very heavy burden.

If we come before God with true sorrow, he will forgive us and will welcome us back with great rejoicing, as we saw in *Dying to*

Live in Jesus' parable of the Prodigal Son. The son had squandered his inheritance and had lived loosely with women but now returned to his father to tell him he was sorry for what he had done. His father ran out to meet him, embraced him and kissed him, gave him the best robe, shoes for his feet and a ring, and celebrated his return with a banquet of a fattened calf, "for this my son was dead, and is alive again; he was lost, and is found" (*Luke* 15:11-24). That is an image of God the Father welcoming back the sinner, no matter how many or how serious the sins he has committed.

We see this too in the Old Testament of the Bible, among other places, in the prophecy of Ezekiel. In answer to those who say that God is not just in his judgment, he replies:

> Hear now, O house of Israel: Is my way not just? Is it not your ways that are not just? When a righteous man turns away from his righteousness and commits iniquity, he shall die for it; for the iniquity which he has committed he shall die. Again, when a wicked man turns away from the wickedness he has committed and does what is lawful and right, he shall save his life. Because he considered and turned away from all the transgressions which he had committed, he shall surely live, he shall not die. Yet the house of Israel says, 'The way of the Lord is not just.' O house of Israel, are my ways not just? Is it not your ways that are not just? (*Ezekiel* 18:25-29)

When God says that the wicked person will die and the righteous will live, he is referring of course to dying in the sense of remaining separated from God for all eternity, and living as being with God forever in heaven. God will always welcome back the sinful person who repents and changes his life. Always. He goes on to say:

> Therefore I will judge you, O house of Israel, every one according to his ways, says the Lord God. Repent and turn from all your transgressions, lest iniquity be your ruin. Cast away from you all the transgressions which you have committed against me, and get yourselves a new heart and a new spirit: Why will you die, O house of Israel? For I have no pleasure in the death of anyone,

says the Lord God; so turn, and live (*Ezekiel* 18:30-32).

Truly, God does not want anyone to be lost forever. He wants all to be saved. He wants his house in heaven to be full. He says this too through St Paul, who writes that God "desires all men to be saved and to come to the knowledge of the truth" (*1 Timothy* 2:4). All we have to do to be saved is to want it, to repent sincerely for our sins, and God in his mercy will welcome us home.

We will be judged by how we have used the gifts God has given us

Another important, exceedingly important, aspect of the judgment is that God will judge each of us by how we have used the various gifts he has given us. What sort of gifts do we mean?

For example, the gift of our family upbringing. Each of us has grown up in a different family situation. Some have been born into a family where their mother and father were united in marriage and the children grew up in a climate of love and lots of happiness, perhaps experiencing too the love of brothers and sisters. That helped them to have stability of character and to be able to use their talents well for the benefit of others. Others did not have the benefit of their parents' stable relationship. Perhaps it was a single-parent family, and they may have experienced lots of arguments, anger, perhaps alcohol abuse and so on. I don't need to describe all the different family situations we may have experienced in growing up, but they do affect how we have lived since our childhood and what we have been able to achieve. It is obvious that in this regard God can expect more from some than from others. That is only right, only just.

There are so many other aspects related to this. For example, we may have grown up in a family where the practice of some religion was an essential part of life, where we learned to worship a higher being and live in accordance with a set of moral principles. Others may have grown up with no such religious belief, or even with hostility towards God and religion, and they were left to their own devices, to discover for themselves how to live.

Some may have enjoyed good health at least most of the time, and others been sick or in pain. Some may have experienced a disability from childhood, or acquired one later through an illness or accident, while others had none. God will judge us by how we have used our health or disability. We all admire greatly those who have been through various forms of adversity and have gone on to achieve great things. God will reward them for that too.

Or take the various talents we have received: intelligence, various manual, musical or sporting skills, a bright personality, the opportunity to attend a good school or university, etc.

Christ himself gives us the well-known parable of the talents, where one person was given five talents, another two and another one. It is an image of God giving different opportunities and abilities to each person and judging them according to how they used them. In the parable, the first person traded with his five talents and made five more, the second made two more and the third buried his talent in order not to lose it and he returned it to his master. In the final reckoning the first two heard the words, "Well done, good and faithful servant; you have been faithful over a little, I will set you over much; enter into the joy of your master." But the one who had not used his one talent to good advantage heard, "You wicked and slothful servant! You knew that I reap where I have not sowed, and gather where I have not winnowed? Then you ought to have invested my money with the bankers, and at my coming I should have received what was my own with interest. So take the talent from him, and give it to him who has the ten talents. For to every one who has will more be given, and he will have abundance; but from him who has not, even what he has will be taken away. And cast the worthless servant into the outer darkness, where there will be weeping and gnashing of teeth" (*Matthew* 25:14-30).

This is summed up in that other familiar statement from the Bible, "Every one to whom much is given, of him will much be required" (*Luke* 12:48). So, we will all be judged in accordance with what we have been given, whether much or little.

The truth that God will expect more from some than from others in the judgment is a great consolation for us. We all know what possibilities we have had in life and we know that other people may have had more or fewer. All God expects is that we use well what he has given us, not that we achieve what some others do. God is fair, he is just. And of course he is always merciful too.

God knows us better than we know ourselves

God, being God, knows everything. Everything: past, present and future. After all, he made everything, and he watches over it in his loving providence. He knows not only the visible aspects of reality but the internal, invisible ones too. Like what we are thinking, how we see reality and why we act the way we do. One of the psalms of the Old Testament describes it:

> O Lord, you have searched me and known me! You know when I sit and when I rise up; you discern my thoughts from afar. You search out my path and my lying down, and are acquainted with all my ways. Even before a word is on my tongue, behold, O Lord, you know it altogether. ... You know me right well. (*Psalm* 139:1-4, 14).

This is also expressed in another book of the Old Testament: "The Lord sees not as man sees; man looks on the outward appearance, but the Lord looks on the heart" (*1 Samuel* 16:7). And St Paul says it too: "It is the Lord who judges me. Therefore do not pronounce judgement before the time, before the Lord comes, who will bring to light the things now hidden in darkness and will disclose the purposes of the heart. Then every man will receive his commendation from

God" (*1 Corinthians* 4:4-5).

In other words, God knows everything about us. He knows us better than we know ourselves. He will judge not only what we did, but why we did it. Others may judge us by what we did, by what they saw, whether good or bad, but God goes beyond that to judge us by our intentions. We may have done a good deed, but perhaps it was motivated by pride, by the desire of being thought well of by others. All of this will be taken into account in the judgment.

And God will judge us not by how our fellow human beings see us, but by how he sees us. This is only fair. And we can thank God for it. Think, for example, of the many times people have misjudged us, judging us harshly and attributing motives to us that we never had. God knows why we did it and he will judge us accordingly. On the other hand, there may have been times when people thought very well of us for something we had done, and we know very well that we had some untoward motive or we had to resort to dishonesty to do it. God will also judge that accordingly.

With all of this, we should not be afraid of the judgment. God is always fair as well as merciful. What we can do to prepare ourselves for the final exam is to be very honest, very sincere with ourselves all the time. Perhaps at the end of each day, we can look back over the day and examine how it went. If we have done something wrong, we should acknowledge it and tell God we are sorry and will try not to do it again. If we have also done good things, we can thank God for them and resolve to keep on doing them. If we live like this we will be well prepared for the judgment. There will be no surprises.

Being honest with ourselves is important, very important. We cannot run away from the truth or gloss over our faults. God sees them and he will judge us by them. He is just as well as merciful. It can be very helpful to recall the story of the American priest Steven Scheier, which we saw in chapter 16 of *Dying to Live*. He had been a priest for twelve years when he was driving home and had a head-on collision which left him seriously injured and unconscious. In that state he had a near-death experience in which he found himself before Jesus Christ in the judgment. He saw his sins, which he acknowledges were unrepented, unconfessed and unforgiven. He says he always had excuses when he committed those sins, but "when talking to Truth personified, alone before the judgment seat, excuses don't exist. No rebuttal is possible. To each offense, I easily agreed. The only thing I could do when Jesus spoke about particular instances in my life was to say internally, 'Yes … Yes, that's true.' When the Lord finished, he said, 'The sentence that you will have for all eternity is hell.' I knew before he even said it what my fate would be. Jesus was doing nothing but honoring my decision. 'I know this is what I deserve,' I thought." That account wakes us up to the reality that the truth will come out in the judgment. There is no hiding it from God. So we should be brutally honest with ourselves now, while there is still time. We should not come with excuses. Before God, before the truth, there is no place for excuses.

God will take into account what we knew or did not know about his law

Perhaps, after reading this book, you say that you have learned many things you had not known about the moral law, the natural law, and that many of your acquaintances have no idea of these matters. Is God going to hold you to account for the sins you committed before you discovered that what you were doing was wrong? And is he going to hold those others to account for what they do not know even now? Of course not. Remember how, in chapter three, we saw how if a person was unaware that a particular act was wrong, God would not hold them to account for it. That would be unjust and God is just, or better, he is justice.

In many areas of life we humans apply the same standard. In families and often in workplaces if someone says he or she did not know that something was wrong, they will not be held accountable for what they did. When it comes to our actions in civil society, however, this may not apply. If we allege we didn't know that something was against the law, the court may very well punish us and remind us that ignorance of the law is no excuse. Before God, obviously, there will be some actions against basic precepts of the natural law which everyone is presumed to know, for example, that killing an innocent person or stealing their property is always wrong. But there can be other lesser-known precepts that many people have not learned, and God will not judge them for that. He is just and merciful.

But let us not presume on God's mercy and fail to learn his law when we have an opportunity to learn it. In reading this book you have already learned the basic precepts of the natural law. You are off to a good start. But you may run into other issues in the future, or you may find yourself in particular situations where you are not sure whether something is right or wrong. Then by all means do what you can to resolve the matter. Read a good book on ethics or ask someone whose judgment you trust. That way you will not come to the final exam only to discover that you did something that you should have known was wrong, and God will hold you to account for it.

What is more, living well pays dividends already in this life. We can only find the happiness we seek when we are obeying God's law and doing what is right. If we are honest and hardworking, faithful to our spouse and children, and we follow the laws of the country, we will have a deep sense of peace, of joy. If, on the contrary, we go against our conscience in matters like these, we will be uneasy, perhaps worried about getting found out. No one wants to live like that.

Naturally too, God will judge each person in accordance with the beliefs and practices of his or her own religion. Some of these beliefs and practices vary widely from one religion to another. So a Muslim will not be judged as if he were a Jew, or a Hindu as if he were a Christian, Except, of course, in the basic principles of the natural law which we are all deemed to know and which oblige everyone.

Getting closer to God

Finally, since we will be meeting God in the judgment, it is a good idea to get to know him well now, while we still have time. And lest we think we have many years to go until we die, no one can have any certainty about that. We don't know when God is going to call us. It could be tomorrow. If we look back at all the exams we have taken in our life, with practically all of them we knew in advance when they were going to be held. We had time to prepare for them. But with the most important exam of all, the final exam, the judgment, we don't know when it will be. So, we have to be prepared all the time.

How can we come to know God better? First, by reading books about him. For Christians, and many others, the Bible is a good start. Especially the New Testament, which gives the life and teachings of Jesus Christ in the four Gospels, plus much more in the other books. Naturally, there are many other books about God and Christ too. Or, if you come from a different religious tradition, the books of your own tradition may be very helpful.

And then, we draw closer to God through prayer, through talking with him and listening to him. Listening to him is very important. He speaks to us in prayer, and often we will hear him telling to do, or not to do, something. Listening to his word in prayer helps us to do what he is asking us, not what we feel like at the time. Prayer also helps us to love God more. He loves us, every single one of us, and it is only natural for us to love him in return. Prayer is a good way to grow in that love. After all, in heaven we are going to experience God's love for all eternity and we can prepare ourselves for it already here on earth. As C.S. Lewis puts it in his book *The Great Divorce,* those who go to heaven begin their heaven on earth.

And, of course, the more we love God the more we will love those around us, both the nice people and those we find difficult. God loves everyone, and so should we. If we live like this, we will be very well prepared for the judgment, for the final exam. Whenever it may be. I will be praying that the reading of this book may help you live a good life and pass the final exam with flying colours in order to reap the reward of eternal happiness. And I ask your prayers for me, that I may be able to give an account of all the gifts God has given me, so I may meet you there.

www.ingramcontent.com/pod-product-compliance
Lightning Source LLC
Chambersburg PA
CBHW070359240426
43671CB00013BA/2568